# THE ADVENTURES OF
# BARON MUNCHAUSEN

The Novel
by
Terry Gilliam & Charles McKeown

æ

Based on the Screenplay
by
Terry Gilliam & Charles McKeown

æ

Based on
THE ADVENTURES OF BARON MUNCHAUSEN
by Rudolf Eric Raspe

æ

Based on the Anecdotes of
Hieronymus Carl Friedrich,
Baron von Munchausen

æ

Illustrated by
James Victore
and
Joyce L. Houlihan

An Applause Original
The Adventures of Baron Munchausen
The Novel

Library of Congress Cataloging-in-Publication Data

Gilliam, Terry.
    The adventures of Baron Munchausen / by Terry Gilliam &
Charles McKeown.
        p.    cm.
    ISBN 1-55783-039-8
    I. McKeown, Charles.   II. Title.
PS3557.I386A64  1989
813'.54--dc19

Published by arrangement with Methuen (London).

APPLAUSE THEATRE BOOK PUBLISHERS
211 West 71st Street
New York, NY  10023
212-595-4735

First Applause printing, 1989

# PROLOGUE

In 1785 Rudolf Eric Raspe, sometime art historian, mining engineer and romantic, sat in London lodgings and wrote down all he could remember of the adventures of his fellow country-man, Baron Munchausen.

The Baron, a soldier of fortune and renowned raconteur, was long since dead and Raspe, exiled in disgrace from his native Hanover and short of funds, may have been tempted to make up a few adventures himself. He hoped to publish them and no one would now be able to challenge their authenticity.

All that he would have to keep in mind was that the adventures should appeal to both frivolous adults and serious children.

Strange as it may seem, while we cannot be certain that all the adventures of Baron Munchausen as set down by Raspe are genuine, we can be sure that by some curious oversight Raspe omitted from his compilation the Baron's most authentic and extraordinary adventure.

# CONTENTS

"... the death sentence would be imposed on
anyone found guilty of cannibalism."

# PART I

# THE SIEGE

*Chaos. Sally amends the posters. The shadow of death.*

## 1

he siege was in its seventh month. The Sultan had put the surrounding countryside to fire and sword, sunk the city's fleet where it lay at anchor in the harbor, and was now encamped with his army outside the city gates.

The siege was effective. The besieged were beginning to starve. For most of them this wasn't new. It had happened before. It would happen again. They had been at war with the Sultan, intermittently, for decades. Nobody could agree what precisely had started it or what might end it. It had, somehow, become just part of life, or, if you were unlucky, death.

A few things had recently changed, however, one of these being the language in which the war was discussed and conducted. The eighteenth century belief in progress and the betterment of the human condition through science, logic and reason had belatedly found its way here. Whereas previous generations of city fathers had spent time muddling through, blaming each other and invoking the local saints, the present government spent time muddling through, blaming each other and invoking words like "progress," "rational," "scientific," "logical," and "order."

It was into this unhappy place, during a temporary truce, that the celebrated Henry Salt Esq. had brought his internationally famous company of travelling players.

2

Sally Salt clambered across piles of rubble and smoldering timber into the square with the monument of the headless horse and headless rider. The air was filled with smoke and dust. Blackened figures moved in all directions. A group of exhausted firemen dragged a fire engine around the edge of the square nearly crushing Sally against a wall. She flattened herself into a doorway. From here, looking up, she saw the warm light from a spectacular sunset fall on a row of bodies hanging by their necks from a gibbet. A badly loaded cart trundled past, shedding a lidless coffin at Sally's feet. She stared at the stale contents. Stretcher parties came and went. An old man and woman, with a small girl about Sally's age in tow, hurried into a side street. The old woman held the girl's arm too tightly and was hurting her. The girl returned Sally's look. Sally fancied she was full of awe and envy at her own grown-up, independent appearance. She practiced one of her scornful stares.

Sally was nine years old. She was small, thin, fragile and bright. In recent weeks, hunger had made her frailer and brighter than ever. Everything that happened to her these days, everything she saw, heard, smelled, touched was exceptionally magical, beautiful, dramatic, and even at the height of the bombardments she wasn't afraid, at least not for herself. She was sensitive to her father's fear, and the fear of the others in the theater company, and she would have liked to protect them. To save them. She would have liked to save the whole town. To defeat the Sultan. If she could manage that then maybe her father would come to appreciate her. For the two years since her mother's death Sally had wanted her father to realize that he could rely on her and draw strength from her.

Leaving the doorway she made her way towards the broken monument in the center of the square. She passed the gigantic horse's head, lying where it had fallen when hit by a cannonball.

Inside it a homeless family had taken refuge and were huddling around a little stack of burning sticks. Sally skipped, to make herself look more like a vulnerable child, and strayed toward the pot in the hope of getting something to eat. Seeing Sally's intention, the woman tending the fire and suckling a baby shook her fist, while the man mending his boots picked up a stone and raised his arm. Sally dodged away.

The pedestal of the damaged statue was covered with official notices instructing citizens in matters of requisitioning,

rationing, curfew arrangements, recruiting, etc. Sally examined a poster which declared that the death sentence would be imposed on anyone found guilty of cannibalism. It was only recently that she'd discovered, to her astonishment, that cannibalism had nothing to do with finding and keeping the cannonballs which the Sultan lobbed over the walls. Moving around the pedestal, Sally saw the notice she was looking for:

### THE THEATRE ROYAL
*THE ADVENTURES OF BARON MUNCHAUSEN*
A Tale Of Incredible Truths, Resurrected and Performed
For The First Time In Thirty Years by
The Henry Salt And Son Players
TICKETS AVAILABLE FROM THE
THEATRE ROYAL BOX OFFICE
Boxes 1s, Pit 6d, Gallery 3d

Taking a piece of charcoal from her pocket, she crossed out 'SON,' and replaced it with 'DAUGHTER.' She stepped back, considered her work with satisfaction, and moved on to an identical poster further along the marble surface.

As the light drained from the town and the fires in the ruins grew correspondingly brighter, a cold, sinister shadow crept across Sally's back. She shuddered, but continued to alter the poster. High on top of the cathedral tower overlooking the square a stone gargoyle in the shape of the angel of death, wings spread, skeletal hands clutching an hourglass and scythe, settled slightly in its bed of coping stones. This movement may have been caused by the effects of continual bombardments and percussive explosions, and yet, had Sally turned around and been able to see through the evening gloom, she might have thought that the carved stone death had more life to it than would normally be considered normal.

*"The truth is, I am the cause of the war!"*

# PART II

# THE THEATER

*The Henry Salt and Son Players. The Right Ordinary Horatio Jackson, theater critic. Jeremy, Rupert, Bill and Desmond try to escape and miss their cue. Salt bemoans his daughter's ability to read. A peculiar character in the square. Salt pays his respects to Jackson and isn't reassured. An old man and his dog interrupt the show. Salt brings down the curtain and loses the end of his nose. Sally makes a new friend. The real Baron Munchausen?*

## 1

t was dark and the evening performance of *The Adventures of Baron Munchausen* as presented by the Henry Salt and Son Players was already under way when Sally returned to the theater. She entered through a hole in the wall where the stage door had once been and stood listening to her father's powerful voice as it boomed at the audience.

"And so, as the sun rose over the island of cheese . . ." From backstage, Sally could hear the mechanical sun grinding up.

" . . . I, Baron Munchausen, who am renowned for telling the truth the whole truth and nothing but the truth . . ."

The audience laughed and jeered. Sally's practiced ear identified this response as friendly.

Having been threatened with the direst consequences if she left the theater, Sally, anxious not to attract attention, climbed the wooden stairs to the back of the stage, carefully avoiding the five noisy treads. At the top she had to wait for Violet and Rose to help each other into their mermaid costumes.

Violet, the oldest member of the company, had once been a great actress, the toast of Paris and London, but at the height of her fame she had killed a rival actress in a duel and seriously injured another. After this her fellow artistes had been reluctant to act with her. Rumor had it she had paid Salt a significant sum to be admitted to the company. Violet tightened the lacing on Rose's mermaid bodice.

"Ouch!"

With the exception of Sally, Rose was the youngest member of the company. She was certainly the prettiest. And now she couldn't breathe.

"Ahhh."

Rose moaned quietly, encouraging Violet to whisper a few words of phoney commiseration into her beautiful shell-like ear.

"How can you become a great actress like me, poor darling, if you get blown to pieces by the Turks? Breathe in." Violet and Rose moved away, enabling Sally to slip into the wings. From here she was able to see the action on stage and, through a gap in the scenery, part of the audience. The auditorium was a wreck. The roof had been blown off weeks before and the orchestra pit was full of fallen masonry, leaving little room for Salt's troupe of traumatized musicians. Above the back of the stalls, smashed plaster figures dangled perilously from the fronts of the few remaining boxes. All of these were now inhabited by people made destitute by the war. People who, to the profound annoyance of Salt, were not in the slightest bit interested in the theater, and who drove the actors crackers by lighting fires, preparing food, hanging out washing, creating babies, and generally making all manner of noise throughout the performances.

The audience in what was left of the stalls consisted in the main of the sick, the halt and the lame; soldiers and civilians who had come to the theater in desperation, seeking a diversion from their suffering.

Sally looked onto the stage and saw her father, illuminated by dozens of candles, wearing old-fashioned clothes, a three-cornered hat with a feather, and a large false nose. He was standing on a piece of scenery painted to resemble a wedge of cheese.

"I bade farewell to my three-legged, horn-headed friends, and prepared to return, across the sea of wine, to my native land."

Here he took a wax apple from his pocket and impaled it on the horn protruding from a monster's head thrust on stage from the wings. He then grasped a length of rope as it descended from the flies, and swung from the 'cheese' onto a miniature galleon revealed when the cheese scenery was dragged off stage. All this, happening in seconds, had taken hours to rehearse. Henry Salt and Son's *Adventures of Baron Munchausen* depended upon fast-moving spectacle, precision timing, and keeping the audience thoroughly bemused. If things didn't go smoothly the show would fail.

Sally watched the sweat pour down her father's face. She knew that he was hating every moment. This "paltry rubbish," as he described the *Adventures of Baron Munchausen*, was a last-ditch attempt to please the local audience and persuade the Municipal Entertainment Committee that the Henry Salt and Son Players were providing a needed service and were worth retaining. The unthinkable alternative, which Salt suspected was being thought in certain quarters, involved the saving of a few food rations by expelling the company from the town. Throwing them on the mercy, or otherwise, of the Sultan. Salt was taking no chances. Having received a lukewarm response to his excellent Shakespeare repertoire, and priding himself on his ability to judge the caliber of an audience, he threw all his energies into producing what he considered to be the silliest, most trivial work which had ever disgraced the bottom of his script box.

Sally had to put on a costume for her appearance in Act Two as one of the Sultan's servants. She was turning from the stage when she was gripped by the arm, swung around, and brought face to face with Daisy.

"Where have you been?"

Sally thought of the girl she had seen in the square and determined not to let Daisy know that she was pinching her arm.

"Eating."

Sally was gratified to see Daisy's eyes widen involuntarily. She too knew how to hurt.

"Roast beef with potatoes . . . Plum pudding with cream."

Daisy began to salivate. She swallowed.

"You little liar! . . . Where?"

"At a banquet. With my friends. On the moon."

Daisy, furious, raised her hand threateningly.

"Behave yourself."

Sally parried:

"You're not my dad," reminding Daisy that she, Sally, was the daughter of Daisy's employer. Daisy hesitated, looking for another tack.

Daisy was about forty years old and as strong as an ox. Salt relied on her for all the heavy jobs which the men in the company refused or were unable to do. She might have been a good actress if she had paid attention to the job instead of producing a steady output of babies, the most recent of which she was now holding.

"The Right Ordinary Horatio Jackson's in tonight! And if he doesn't like us he'll throw us to the Turks!"

Daisy rotated Sally and pointed her in the direction of a box on the opposite side of the forestage. There, surrounded by generals, functionaries and emissaries, sat Horatio Jackson, examining official papers and occasionally scrutinizing the stage. He looked pleasant enough. Sally noted his clean and tidy appearance. Jackson prided himself on being a sane, rational, reasonable man. He was famous for it. He turned to Hardy, his ever-present secretary.

"The point is, is this theater viable, and, stroke, or, are these actors fulfilling a useful and, stroke, or, necessary, function?"

Hardy nodded and shook his head. Sally and Daisy, from the other side of the stage, watched Jackson carefully, trying to lip-read.

Meanwhile, on stage a few yards away, things were not proceeding as they ought. Salt was unmistakably flustered.

"We heaved anchor and set sail!"

A certain emphatic quality in his voice, taken with the fact that it had suddenly risen an octave, left the listener in little doubt that something was amiss. He glanced furtively at Jackson and then, desperately, into the wings.

"We heaved anchor and set sail!"

His voice had climbed another octave. In less than half a minute Salt had travelled from baritone to countertenor. Still nothing happened.

"Get on with it, skipper!"

The voice from the back of the stalls was joined by others.

"He's becalmed!"

"There's been a mutiny!"

Laughter. The audience, to Salt's dismay, was beginning to show real signs of enjoyment.

Beneath the stage, unaware of Salt's predicament directly above their heads, Jeremy, Rupert, Bill and Desmond, the hard core of the company, were preparing for their scene and taking measures to escape. Bill, who was black and six feet seven inches tall, stood in a deep narrow trench shoveling out lumps of earth. Throwing down the shovel he slumped, exhausted, against the side of the hole.

"Come on, somebody else have a go!"

"You want to escape or don't you?"

Jeremy, the dwarf, daubed a streak of pink make-up onto his big false ears.

"This'll take years! It's solid clay down here!"

So far Bill was the only one to have done any digging and he resented the others assuming that just because he was strong he was suited to the kind of work normally left to Daisy. Desmond, whose idea it had been to dig themselves out, straightened his leg padding.

"I dug my way out of the 1789 Black Forest Miracle-cycle Festival single-handed, and that was on granite."

Nobody was ever sure whether Desmond was the most intelligent or the silliest member of the company.

Light suddenly flooded into the understage gloom as a door opened and Sally dropped into view.

"The waves! The waves!"

The group below stage were instantly galvanized into action and flew to large wooden handles which they began turning vigorously.

"We're actors! Where the devil are the stage hands?" Rupert was used to better things.

"Dead."

Bill had ceased to be his usual cheerful self about a month before.

"They can't all have been killed!"

Rupert swung his handle angrily. He was looking for someone to blame. A tendency of his which always provoked Jeremy.

"Not killed, ducky, suicide."

He caught Rupert's eye and smiled innocently.

"Nothing whatever to do with your acting."

Sally returned to stage level, where the waves had now begun to work and Daisy, tussling in the wings with a capstan, a series of rope pulleys and a wind machine, was making Salt's galleon rock back and forth and sail unsteadily through the waves. Salt's voice had returned almost to normal.

"But ill-luck pursued me. I was blown towards the waiting jaws of a whale of such prodigious length that even with a telescope I could not see the end of him."

As Salt raised his telescope, a small two-dimensional whale appeared from the wings and moved along the back row of waves, exiting on the opposite side. At this point, another, larger cut-out whale emerged behind the middle row of waves and moved across the stage in the opposite direction to the first, giving the impression, or rather intending to give the impression, that it was all one fish and that it was drawing closer to the Baron. Now a huge fish's mouth came on behind the front row of waves and snapped shut, eclipsing Salt and his 'galleon' from view. Following this Violet and Rose entered as mermaids and sang, very nearly in unison.

"What will become of the Baron?
Surely this time there is no escape!
What will become of the Baron?
Surely this time there is no escape!"

This was saved from utter banality by the singers' passionate attempts to upstage one another. Salt poked his head out between the fish's jaws and addressed the audience.

"I have learned from experience that a modicum of snuff can be most efficacious."

Here he mimed taking a pinch of snuff from a snuff-box and scattering it around the fish's mouth. The fish's head began to shudder, Salt ducked back 'inside,' the musicians provided an appropriate crescendo, and Salt was hauled out on a wire from behind the top of the fish as if being jettisoned through its blowhole. He was then lowered to the stage, pretending to float down on his coattails.

All in all, considering the shortage of man-power and materials and the generally appalling conditions in which they were working, the Henry Salt and Son Players could have been said to be putting on an extremely impressive show. As the curtain fell on Act I, Salt took his bow to scant, apathetic applause.

In Horatio Jackson's box at the side of the stage, Hardy breathed obsequiously over his master's shoulder.

"Are you enjoying it, sir?"

Jackson pondered the question for a moment.

"Am I enjoying it?"

He was always scrupulous when it came to distinguishing work from pleasure.

"I don't think that's a question which falls within the parameters of our enquiry, is it?"

Hardy shook his head in agreement.

Onstage, behind the curtain, Sally watched her father rant and rave.

"Damn and blast! Where are the waves? The waves!"

Jeremy, Rupert and Desmond cowered behind Bill's massive bulk and pushed him forward from the understage opening. Salt was grateful for a target.

"You incompetent imbecile!"

"It wasn't my fault!"

What Bill lacked as a natural fall guy, he more than made up for in chivalry.

"It was her!"

He thrust a large index finger at Daisy, who was slumped, gasping for breath, over her wind machine.

"It wasn't me, it was him!"

Daisy's ferocious scream started the baby crying, and for a moment it looked as if she was going to hit Bill with it.

"You big pintle!"

Salt stepped between them, exasperated at not being able to vent his anger without becoming a peacemaker.

"We're supposed to be professionals!"

Instantly, Salt regretted having said this, as it flashed through his mind that professionals got paid and that it might not be a good thing, just at the moment, to remind his company that for the past two months they hadn't been.

"If we're professionals how come you don't pay us?"

From time to time Salt hated Desmond.

"We're trying to stay alive."

This was the truth. Salt caught sight of Sally.

"Sally!"

He stepped briskly towards her.

Sally felt that she understood her father well. She knew that he was a good man. She knew that under his bluster he was weak. She knew that at the moment he was relieved to be able to latch onto the role of anxious father in order to escape from his other problems. She slid between flats of scenery, ran to the back of the stage and hid. Salt chased and caught her.

"Where have you been?"

"Nowhere."

Sally cherished her secrets.

"Don't lie to me."

"I'm not."

Salt had no intention of being drawn into a childish philosophical swamp about the meanings of words. He took Sally's hand and marched her towards his dressing room.

"Don't you think I've got enough to worry about?"

"I was . . ."

"Yes, I know, playing with dragons, wrestling with angels . . . Wandering mindlessly through exploding shells and blazing buildings."

Sally didn't know whether to feel indignant or thankful that her father so misunderstood her. Nearing his dressing room they came upon a group of soldiers who were tearing the canvas from scenery and dismantling props to make a splint for a wounded comrade's leg. Salt's face changed color.

"Stop that! Put those down! Don't you dare!"

He let go of Sally and began grappling with the soldiers.

"This scenery has appeared before every crowned head in Europe!"

The kind of name-dropping that Salt went in for didn't require names. The soldiers pushed him away, unimpressed.

"You philistines! These are the props for *Antony and Cleopatra!*"

Salt was on the verge of tears. The soldiers ignored him.

"I shall report you! Oafs! Ignoramuses!"

He flinched as a piece of painted canvas was torn into strips.

"You don't deserve art! You don't deserve theater!"

One of the soldiers smiled and sank his teeth into an artificial pear.

"That's the fruit from *Hamlet*! Is nothing sacred? All right! Go on! I hope you choke to death!"

Salt grabbed Sally and yanked her into his dressing room. This was the only undamaged room in the building. The walls were covered with theater posters of Henry Salt and Son's past productions in all the great cities of Europe. Above Salt's desk hung a portrait of his late wife, Sally's mother. Salt fell into his chair.

"What in heaven's name is the world coming to?"

Sally recognized this as one of those silly questions which aren't supposed to get an answer.

"Stay in the theater or I shall have to lock you up."

She looked at the posters.

"Where's my brother?"

"What?"

Salt was dumbfounded.

"You haven't got a brother."

"Then why does it say 'Henry Salt and *Son*'? I'm your daughter."

Salt never ceased to be amazed at Sally's capacity to amaze him.

"We should never have taught you to read!"

Catching sight of himself in a small cracked mirror he took off his false nose which was tied round the back of his head with elastic.

"*And Son* is traditional. That's the way it's supposed to be."

His composure was returning. Sally knew she was in for the not-so-potted history of the Henry Salt and Son Players. Salt, leaning past Sally to fasten the warped door, saw beyond it two cane baskets making their way across the stage, apparently of their own volition. He rocketed out of his chair and shot from the dressing room like a demented greyhound leaving its trap.

Overtaking the baskets on the far side of the stage, he flung open their lids, revealing Jeremy and Rupert in one and Desmond and Bill in the other.

"Get out of there! Get out! You scoundrels! You traitors!"

It wasn't in Salt's nature to interpret this idiosyncratic escape attempt as a cry for help.

"Run away in our darkest hour, would you?"

"Yes."

Desmond again. Salt scowled.

"You weak-kneed, lily-livered . . ."

He hesitated, just long enough for Jeremy to come in.

"Yellow-bellied?"

Salt glanced suspiciously at Jeremy's open guileless face.

"Thank you. Yellow-bellied lot! You give theater a bad name! You give actors a bad name! You give escaping a bad name! Where the blazes did you think you could escape to? Eh?"

Rupert crossed his eyes and pointed simultaneously in opposite directions. A gesture which made him feel better but which earned him a clout round the ear. Salt, pulling himself up to his rather short, full height, resonated imperiously.

"Get back to your dressing rooms and prepare for Act Two."

2

In the square of the bronze monument of the headless horse with the headless rider, an old man tottered up to one of the posters advertising *The Adventures of Baron Munchausen* and peered at it myopically. He was tall, though stooped, and wore faded old-fashioned clothes and a three-cornered hat with a feather, and a sword. He was accompanied by an equally ancient dog. The old man's large beaky nose almost touched the poster as

he read it, growled angrily, tore it from the wall, threw it onto
the ground and stomped purposefully away.


3

Towards the end of the interval, Salt thought it wise to pay
his respects to the Right Ordinary Horatio Jackson and
apologize for the hiatus in Act One. Jackson's box continued to
be packed with important officials and Salt had difficulty in
getting in. However, Hardy, noticing Salt hovering at the door,
spoke to Jackson and then beckoned him forward. Salt forced his
way through the crush of bodies to where he could see Jackson
put his signature on a sheet of paper and hand it to Hardy.

"The Sultan's demands are still not sufficiently rational. The
only lasting peace will be one based upon reason and scientific
principle." Hardy folded and sealed the document and handed it
to a waiting emissary who, turning, collided with Salt.

Having chosen to wear his false nose, for fear of not
otherwise being recognized, Salt now felt confident in
removing it and, stretching the elastic, he set it onto his
forehead. An awful, over-muscular smile spread across his face.

"I'm most terribly sorry, your Right Ordinariness . . . Our
first act didn't quite go as well as we would have liked . . . One
or two little . . ."

Jackson smiled pleasantly and held up his hand.

"Please don't apologize, Mr. Salt. You're doing your best in
difficult circumstances."

Salt was overjoyed. Perhaps he'd misjudged Jackson. He was
about to launch into a long series of ornate compliments which
he'd rehearsed beforehand when Jackson's attention was
diverted by the arrival of two soldiers supporting a wounded
officer. Hardy looked at Jackson and then waved them forward.

"Excuse me a moment."

Jackson bowed slightly to Salt as he was given a piece of

paper by Hardy. He read this rapidly and looked up at the wounded officer.

"So, you're the officer who risked his life by single-handedly destroying six enemy cannon and rescuing ten of our men captured by the Turks?"

"Yes, sir."

The wounded man was clearly in pain.

"The officer about whom we've heard so much?"

The officer looked down, modestly.

"I suppose so, sir."

Jackson smiled and glanced at Hardy.

"Always taking risks far beyond the call of duty."

"I do my best, sir."

Salt couldn't believe his luck. This was wonderful. Not only had he been well received by Jackson, but his visit had coincided with a happy moment. Salt knew there were benefits to being linked, in the minds of the powerful, with success and celebration. Jackson gazed serenely over his half-glasses.

"Have him executed at once. This sort of behavior is demoralizing for the ordinary soldiers and citizens who are leading normal, simple, unexceptional lives."

The soldiers holding the wounded officer saluted and took him away. Jackson turned to Hardy.

"Things are difficult enough without these emotional people rocking the boat."

Hardy nodded, then shook his head as more emissaries

arrived with fresh dispatches.

Salt was stunned. From time to time he was given to being visited at four o'clock in the morning by the thought that he was a vain, foolish, ignorant man whose life and work were completely worthless. And now, here, at eight-thirty in the evening, a time when he was usually at his most optimistic, a similar abyss had opened before him. Seeing that Jackson had once again become immersed in paperwork, Salt replaced his false nose in the middle of his face and edged carefully out of the box.

### 4

When the musicians struck up and the curtains opened on the second act of *The Adventures of Baron Munchausen*, Sally, dressed as one of the Sultan's servants in a pink turban with matching bolero and baggy Turkish trousers, was waiting in the wings. She didn't have any lines to say and she was bored with the show, but she would bring on trays of pretend food and drink and carry off pretend messages competently.

On stage, Daisy, Rose and Violet danced, Turkish style, around the set of the Sultan's palace as Salt, in his Baron Munchausen regalia, was lowered from the flies on a small platform fixed behind a two-dimensional cloud.

"Ahh . . . Constantinople! The court of the Grand Turk! What a surprise that a passing zephyr should waft me here. Perhaps fate wishes me to teach the Sultan a lesson or two."

A few cheers and hisses from the audience set Salt glancing nervously towards Jackson, who was paying no attention. He stepped off his cut-out cloud and walked to the front of the stage as the Sultan, played by Peter the actor, entered holding a bottle of wine. Salt acknowledged him and then addressed the audience.

"His Highness the Sultan loved good wine and could never resist a wager. Characteristics that were to cost him dear."

*"She would have liked to save the whole town."*

Sally's mind began to wander. As her father's voice droned on, she began to invent her own plot and dialogue in which she saw herself stopping the show and presenting her own version, to the admiration and gratitude of all. In the midst of this reverie she became aware that something unrehearsed was happening. Her first thought was that she had missed her cue, and her heart echoed the thought by missing a beat. Then she realized that the voice she was hearing wasn't her father's. It was, in fact, a hoarse, cracked voice, and it seemed to be coming from the back of the auditorium. Sally squinted cautiously around the edge of the scenery. In the dim light she saw an old man with a thin dog staggering down the aisle towards the stage. He was waving a walking stick and shouting.

"Lies! Lies! Lies! Lies! . . . Stop this travesty!"

On stage the music and dancing stopped. Only Salt's mouth continued to move, but no sound emerged. As the old man proceeded through the stalls the audience began to murmur. Jackson, always sensitive to shifts of mood among large groups of people, spoke to Hardy.

"Is this supposed to happen?"

Hardy shook his head.

"Er, yes, sir, I should think so."

5

Onstage, Salt was valiantly trying to get the show going again and, against the odds, win the audience's attention from the old man who was now glowering up at him from the front of the stalls.

"One day, after a sumptuous dinner, the Sultan bade me accompany him to his private apartments."

Here the old man began to climb the steps at the side of the orchestra pit onto the stage. He seemed driven by demonic energy.

"This man's an impostor!"

He jabbed towards Salt with his stick.

"I am Baron Munchausen! . . . And I won't be made a fool of!"

"Please! You cannot come up here!"

Salt screeched at him in a harsh whisper.

"You are presenting a mockery!"

The old man stepped across the footlight candles and onto the stage. His dog followed.

"You present me as if I were a ridiculous fiction! A joke! I won't have it!"

Sally realized that this interruption probably spelled disaster, but at the same time she couldn't help enjoying it. She watched, fascinated. Now that the old man was in the light she could see him more clearly. He was tall, thin, had a large beaky nose, a small pointed beard, a turned-up moustache and a pigtail. He wore a long black cloak over a faded red coat-jacket, a three-cornered hat with a feather, and black silk breeches. Sally was amazed. Except for his height, he looked exactly like her father's Baron Munchausen, which Salt had copied from an illustration in their battered old script. She knew he couldn't be the real Baron Munchausen. To begin with, there could never have been any such person. And if there had been, he'd certainly be dead by now. Sally looked at the old man as Salt pushed him back towards the edge of the stage and wished that, just for once, she might be wrong.

Not for the first time this evening, Salt, his brain boiling with fury, could hear the audience laughing, jeering, and apparently positively enjoying themselves. What was the matter with them? He vowed to himself that if he ever got out of this town alive, he'd never return. They could beg and plead with him until the cows came home. He had almost succeeded in propelling the idiot intruder back into the stalls when the old man, drawing his sword, inadvertently sliced the end off Salt's false nose, revealing the real one nesting inside it. The audience roared its approval as Salt leaped back waving frantically at his actors.

"Get him off! For heaven's sake! Get him off!"

Peter the actor ran off stage. Desmond, Jeremy, Bill and Rupert looked at one another doubtfully, advanced one step, and then hastily retreated as the old man lurched towards them swirling his sword. The weight of the sword carried him into the wings where he lost his balance and sliced through a rope, sending a chandelier crashing into the middle of the stage. It was here that Salt felt the need for drastic measures.

"Tabs! Tabs! Bring in the tabs!"

The curtains closed, causing uproar in the audience. On stage Salt was apoplectic.

"Get off! Get off! You cretinous old fool! You're ruining the show!"

Salt made another attempt to get hold of the old man, but was driven back by the snarling old dog.

"Down boy, down!"

Sally came out of the wings and patted the dog on the head. It licked her hand. Salt shook his fists in the air.

"Somebody get rid of him! Quick! Get him out of here! Bill, Jeremy, Desmond! Do something!"

A missile from the audience hit the other side of the curtain.

"I must speak to the audience."

Salt bolted round the side of the curtain and onto the forestage where he tried to soothe the impatient mob.

"Er, ladies and gentlemen."

He forced himself not to peep at Jackson.

"We are most dreadfully sorry about this unfortunate occurrence. Please, I give you my assurance that we will continue soon with . . ."

6

As Salt spoke to the audience, a curious scene was taking place behind the curtain. The old man, exhausted now, was peering at the actresses. Rose was made uncomfortable by this close scrutiny.

"Hello!"

She moved behind Daisy, who thrust her baby forward as if expecting it to protect her.

"Hello!"

The old man seemed confused.

"Beautiful ladies, yes. Beautiful ladies . . . "

Violet, not being of the shrinking variety, thrust her chest under the old man's chin.

"What good taste you have."

But the old man gave the impression of seeing something else. Something which no one else saw.

"But otherwise, it's all quite wrong."

He stared at Sally, who was stroking the dog. Sally smiled. She was going to like him. He looked so funny. Everyone else was against him. She would be his friend. His only friend. Besides the dog. Just as he would be her only friend. Besides the dog. From in front of the curtain Salt could still be heard ingratiating himself with the audience. Desmond leaned apprehensively towards the old man.

"Eh, listen Cocky, we've got a show to do."

The old man glanced at Desmond and then did a double take.

"Good lord! Berthold!"

His face lit up.

"I'm not really Berthold, I'm just playing Berthold!" Desmond couldn't stand mentally defective fans.

"The name's Desmond, get it?"

Undeterred, the old man clasped Desmond in a messy but

firm embrace.

"How on earth! . . . It's marvelous to see you! . . . How are you? . . . Where have you been? . . . How are your legs? . . . Where are the others?"

Looking around, he focused on Bill, Rupert, and Jeremy, seeing them now, apparently, for the first time.

"Albrecht! Adolphus! Gustavus! . . . I don't believe it! This is miraculous!"

Bill, Rupert and Jeremy looked perplexed.

"I'm Bill."

"He's Bill."

Jeremy rarely agreed with Bill, but this, obviously, wasn't the time for dissent. At this point, Salt returned from in front of the curtain.

"Is he still here?! Get rid of him!"

Before anybody had a chance to continue not doing what Salt told them to do, Jackson, escorted by Hardy and a group of generals, walked onto the stage.

"Is anything the matter?"

Jackson always contrived to simulate an open mind. A picture of the wounded officer in Jackson's box flashed through Salt's frenzied brain.

"I'm terribly sorry, sir. We're about to begin the second act again. Any moment now, sir. If you would just . . . "

"Who is this?"

Jackson waved a finger at the old man.

"I've no idea! Some old, useless lunatic!"

If Jackson was going to insist on having someone else shot, Salt was ready with a candidate.

"He's Baron Munchausen."

Sally had decided to pretend to believe that the old man was indeed Baron Munchausen. She was, after all, supposed to be a child. Why not make the most of it? The old man smiled and bowed to her. Salt looked daggers and raised his finger to his lips. Jackson looked at Sally as if she'd just arrived from another planet. Then, remembering that his more populist speeches always contained a brief homily on the importance of the family, in which he observed that without children the whole concept of progress was rendered null and void, he permitted a condescending smile to rearrange his features.

"I see. The *real* Baron Munchausen."

Hardy and the generals, picking up on the paternal tone, all frowned warmly. The old man straightened his back.

"Yes, indeed. And who, sir, may I ask, are you?"

"A public servant."

Being modest was one of Jackson's favorite ostentations.

"I am responsible, among other things, for the licensing of this theater."

"This, sir, is the Right Ordinary Horatio Jackson, who just happens to be winning the war and saving the city."

Salt could think of no occasion when laying it on thick had been the wrong thing to do.

"Pah!"

The old man's nostrils flared.

"He's an ass! Only I can end this war!"

Sally stopped petting the dog. For the first time today she began to feel frightened. Frightened for the old man. Jackson rearranged his face indulgently and adjusted his glasses.

"Explain yourself?"

"I can end it because I began it. I am the cause."

Jackson's eyes showed boredom.

"I'm afraid, sir, you have a rather weak grasp of reality."

"*Your* reality, sir, is lies and balderdash, and I'm delighted to say that I have no grasp of it whatsoever!"

The old man spat this out with renewed energy. Sally didn't know what it meant, but she was sure that he was right. Jackson pulled out his watch.

"This man needs a doctor."

"Doctor?! Doctor?!"

The old man spun around, alarmed. Salt moved forward.

"We'll see to it, sir. And now, if you would like to resume your seat, we'll continue with the show."

Jackson nodded and, followed by his entourage, left the stage. Salt turned to the intruder, flapping his arms.

"Off! Off! Off!"

Again, the dog drove him away.

"Please! If we don't get on with it they'll throw us to the Turks! Be reasonable!"

"*I* will 'get on with it'!"

To everyone's astonishment, the old man threw off his cloak and, before anyone could prevent him, limped around the side of the curtain and onto the forestage from where he began to address the audience.


# 7

"My lords, ladies and gentlemen, Baron Munchausen at your service."

He bowed stiffly. The audience, delighted, began to cheer and shout.

"Give us another tune on your saber!"

The old man carried on, confidently.

"Most of you won't remember me, or my adventures . . . but I assure you they are true."

This really got the audience going.

"True, eh?"

"That's the stuff!"

"Pull the other one!"

"Come on, let's have the truth!"

"Quick, before you drop dead!"

Jackson, furious that his sensible instructions were not being followed, ordered his generals to go onstage and pull the old man off. The audience went wild.

"Leave him alone!"

"We want the Baron!"

Hesitating, the generals looked to Jackson.

"Let him be!"

"Let the old geezer alone!"

Seeing the audience was against him, Jackson signalled the generals to retreat.

"Hurrah!"

"Victory!"

"We got the Baron!"

The audience clapped and threw their bandages in the air. Jackson smiled and waved, giving the impression that he understood their applause to be meant for him. The old man straightened his waistcoat.

"The truth is, I am the cause of the war!"

There was a moment's near silence before a fat man in the middle of the stalls stood up, laughing.

"Don't be daft!"

The woman behind him pulled him back into his seat.

"What about the Turks then?"

"You're the cause of the border dispute, are you?"

A young man minus a hand laughed and waved his bandaged stump.

"What border dispute?"

This was the captain of one of the ships now lying at the bottom of the harbor.

"It's the sea routes we're fighting for!"

A woman with singed hair spoke from the other side of the aisle. She was toothless and almost unintelligible.

"No it isn't! It's because we refused to pay the tribute money!"

"That was the last time!"

A man in good quality clothes kicked the bench in front of him.

"It's because they insulted us!"

"How?"

"He doesn't know!"

The toothless woman, who loved speaking in public, got to her feet and proceeded to spray those around her with droplets of saliva.

"It's my opinion that their ears are set too close together! And that's always a bad sign!"

"Heads! Heads!"

A legless soldier hauled himself with powerful arms across two empty seats.

"How can their ears be set too close together unless their heads are too narrow?"

This particular observation seemed to strike a chord and several groups in the audience took up the chant.

"Their heads are too narrow! Their heads are too narrow!"

Sally, with the other actors, stood behind the curtain listening, transfixed, to what was going on out front. The old man brought the audience to order.

"You poor deluded fools!"

The arguing, shouting and fighting stopped.

"If you will only do me the courtesy of accepting the word of a gentleman, I will reveal the true cause of the war."

The old man drew his sword and flourished it, having the effect, as if by magic, of causing the curtains to open. Sally and the others dived for the wings. The old man waited impatiently for the stage to empty, then proceeded.

"After my return from Egypt, I was warmly welcomed by the Grand Turk, His Highness the Sultan, who knew of my reputation and held me in high esteem. In fact, so delighted was he with my company that he offered me access to his harem."

Here he gave a little chuckle.

"One day, the Sultan brought me a bottle of his favorite Tokay wine."

Backstage, Sally watched her father and the other actors reel in panic. The old man had launched them into some approximate version of Act Two. He seemed, more or less, to know the lines. It was uncanny. Could he really be the Baron? Or some reincarnation? Not possible. But what did it mean? And if they began to follow his directions, where might it end? On the other hand, if they refused to cooperate with this person who had appropriated their show, the audience, frustrated beyond endurance, might tear them to pieces. Not to mention their fate if they continued to run foul of Jackson.

These questions were settled by there being no time to consider them, and Peter the actor made his entrance as the Sultan and strode, trembling with fear, down towards the old man at the footlights. Sally, as the Sultan's servant, stepped briskly out behind him. She too was nervous but, unlike the others, she was also exhilarated.

By the time Peter the actor reached the forestage, he seemed to Sally to have been transformed into the real Sultan. Waiting for him under the proscenium arch, the old man too appeared to have changed. He'd become young and vigorous. Perhaps he'd really become the real Baron Munchausen?

Salt, not quite yet a convert to this view of things, leaned out from behind the scenery and yanked Sally off the stage. He didn't intend to let her get involved in what might turn out to be a catastrophe.

But Sally was already far gone. She watched, from the wings, "The Sultan's Tale," told brilliantly by her real Baron Munchausen and enacted by him with the, at first hesitant, participation of the Henry Salt and Son Players.

*"Well, time's nearly up, I think."*

# PART III

# THE SULTAN'S TALE

*A wager. Berthold removes his weights and shows his mettle. The Sultan's nasty opera. The executioner's assistant prepares the Baron's neck. Bucephalus, Adolphus, Gustavus and Albrecht lend a hand. Berthold returns in the nick of time. The Baron collects his winnings. His Highness is not amused.*

## 1

he Sultan filled two glasses from the bottle he was holding, gave one to me, touched my glass with his own and sipped the contents thoughtfully.

"What do you think of that, eh?"

I took a second sip and glanced at one of the extremely large ladies who occupied most of the space in the harem.

"Not bad."

"Not bad?"

The Sultan looked aghast.

"My dear Munchausen, it's impossible to find better."

I smiled.

"Humbug, Your Majesty! What will you wager that I don't provide you, within the hour, with a bottle of Tokay far superior to this from the imperial cellar at Vienna, a mere thousand odd miles away? Accept my challenge. If I don't succeed you may cut off my head."

I flicked a speck of dust from the sleeve of my coat.

"These are my stakes. What are yours?"

"I accept."

Having been educated at one of the best English public schools, the Sultan was extremely competitive.

"And if you succeed, you may take from my treasury as much treasure as the strongest man can carry."

As far as I was concerned the treasure was already mine.

"Agreed."

I twirled my moustache.

"Give me pen and ink and I'll write to the Empress immediately."

While the Sultan sent for pen and ink I skirted around a handsome tiger on a bed of flowers and picked my way through foothills of female flesh to a trellissed window. Opening part of the trellis I leaned out and shouted in the direction of a courtyard below.

"Berthold!"

My servants Berthold, Gustavus, Adolphus, and Albrecht were sitting beside a fountain, playing cards. Berthold was remarkable for his incredibly muscular legs, Gustavus was very short but possessed an enormous chest and ears, Adolphus had long-range eyesight which he kept under control with thick-lensed glasses, and Albrecht was black and towered over everyone else even when he was the only one sitting down.

Berthold waved to me and hobbled into the palace dragging two heavy weights, one attached to each ankle. These were designed to slow him down to normal speed, enabling him to enjoy a reasonably long conversation without inadvertently shooting off at a thousand miles an hour in the middle of it. Gustavus, who was particularly fond of telling jokes, had in past years been deeply demoralized by Berthold's tendency to disappear before the punch line, and it had been he who had suggested the ankle weights.

I was signing my letter to the Empress Marie Theresa as Berthold heaved his weighted legs into the harem, attracting as he did so the admiration of the concubines who were all much taken with the muscularity of his nether regions. I folded the letter and sealed it.

"Take this to Vienna, to the Empress. She'll give you a bottle of Tokay. Bring it straight back to me."

"Right oh."

Berthold put the letter into his pocket and unfastened his leg weights, keeping a firm grip on them while he oriented himself in the direction of the exit. I moved back a pace. Berthold released the weights and instantly began to run so fast that his whirling legs dug a small trench in the tiled harem floor before getting a grip and propelling him through the door.

The Sultan and I rushed to the trellissed window from where we saw what could only have been Berthold flash away from the palace and disappear over the horizon leaving a thin trail of dust. The Sultan turned from the window and looked ruefully at his ruined floor. This would mean a return of the builders. He opened a drawer in a small inlaid table, lifted out a beautifully carved hourglass and, gazing steadily at me, set it up, dramatically, where we could both observe the sand running out. I responded by taking, simultaneously, a miniature hourglass from my waistcoat pocket, inverting it, and replacing it. The Sultan smiled happily.

"Perhaps you would care for some entertainment while you wait. I've been composing a short opera. Would you like to hear a song or two?"

"No thank you."

I was familiar with the Sultan's musical proclivities.

"You'll love it."

The Sultan flexed an elbow and a group of guards hurried away to return moments later pushing what looked like a very large and heavy organ console with keyboard, stops and foot pedals. My curiosity was aroused. The instrument had no visible pipes, and in spite of my great knowledge of such matters, I found myself unable to predict precisely what kind of sound it might make. The Sultan seated himself at the keyboard.

"It's a comedy. It's called The Torturer's Apprentice. Here's the overture."

He began to play, producing the most astonishing and disturbing noise I had ever heard. It was half mechanical and half human. It seemed that the instrument maker had set out to reproduce the human voice and then changed his mind. I was about to interrupt the Sultan and congratulate him on his ownership of this new and innovative instrument and suggest that perhaps more development work needed doing when the lid of the console opened and a thin hand reached out. To my horror, one of the guards lifted the lid and smashed it down hard, crushing the hand and causing it to retreat back into the body of the instrument. The Sultan continued, unconcerned.

"Now the curtain rises on a typical everyday torture chamber. Yosrick, the young apprentice, sings of his joy in his job."

The Sultan began to sing, accompanying himself with the infernal music from the organ.

"A torturer's apprentice went his
merry way to work one day.
I bend and stretch and ply my trade,
Making people all afraid,
But things look black,
Business is slack,
There's no one in the rack but me."

The Sultan stopped playing and turned to me. A single semi-human note continued from the instrument. He swung around and hit one of the stops. The note ceased abruptly. The Sultan looked serious.

"There's something of a recession in his business, you see, owing to the spread of various nauseating liberal sentiments. In fact, he has only one victim that day, a beautiful seventeen-year-old girl whom he recognizes in a rack song as his old playmate Griselda."

The Sultan began to play again, furiously working the pedals. This produced, from a corner of the box, a screaming operatic woman's voice.

"Ah. Ah. Ah. Ah. Ah.
Oh. Oh. O. OO. Oh.
Ah. Ah. Ah. Ah. Ah."

The Sultan responded.

"Is it you?"

The voice replied.

"It is me!"

"Is it you?"

"It is me!"

"You, you, you."

"Me, me, me."

"Oh, horror! Torn between his love, his job and her fingernails!"

I got up and, looking through a grille in the back of the instrument, discovered what didn't in the least surprise me. Half a dozen poor devils were crammed inside. Here, they were forced to make 'music' in response to the knife blades, hammers and spiked wheels which hurt them on a diatonic scale whenever the Sultan manipulated the appropriate control. I returned to my cushion in disgust, determined to take revenge on the Sultan on behalf of all his unfortunate victims.

Awakened from a shallow sleep by a fat sweaty man with a large shiny scimitar and recognizing the blind executioner, I checked the hourglass. The upper chamber was almost empty of sand. I confirmed this with my own pocket version and calculated that I had only five minutes left. The executioner's assistant began to measure and prepare my neck, drawing a dotted line around it, while the Sultan, concerned that I should hear the whole of his opera before being put to death, pushed on enthusiastically.

"Act Four is set in an abattoir. I see a lot of slapstick. We begin with the arrival of the Eunuchs' chorus who sing:

Cut off in my prime,

Surrounded by beautiful women all the time,
A Eunuch's life is hard,
A Eunuch's life is hard,
A Eunuch's life is hard,
And nothing else."
I stood up, pushing away the executioner's assistant.
"Excuse me a moment!"
The Sultan played on.
"Oh, you mustn't miss this aria! It reminds me of my school days in England.

Life is rather like a game,
It's important that you win,
And though it is a terrible shame,
If you lie and cheat and sin,
Play up and play the game . . ."
I whistled sharply. Moments later a magnificent white stallion galloped into the harem scattering guards, servants and concubines. I leaped into the saddle.
"Back in four minutes!"
I wheeled the horse around, hurdled a couple of concubines and jumped clean through the trellissed window.

## 2

Adolphus, Gustavus and Albrecht, sitting playing cards by the fountain, received the Baron plummeting into their midst on Bucephalus as if it happened every day of the week. This was indeed almost the case. Exposure over many years to the Baron's extraordinary adventures had made them blasé to anything as mundane as this present descent on horseback from a mere seventy feet onto paving stones and with no safety net. The Baron patted Bucephalus.
"Where the hell's Berthold?"
"Dunno."

Gustavus picked up a card.

"I thought he was with you."

Albrecht threw in another coin, raising the stakes.

"If he's not back in about three and a half minutes the Sultan's going to cut off my head!"

"And?"

Adolphus liked, occasionally, to tease the Baron.

"And?!"

The Baron was flabbergasted. Adolphus winked at Gustavus.

"Is that all? . . . I'm sorry, but I don't really find that funny."

He turned to Albrecht.

"Do you find that . . . ?"

The Baron broke in, exasperated.

"This isn't a joke! It's a wager!"

One of the Baron's famous wagers was guaranteed to concentrate the minds of his followers. They leaped to their feet and responded in unison.

"A wager!"

This was an inside joke. Gustavus flung himself onto his stomach and pressed a large ear to the ground.

"He's asleep! I can hear him snoring! About nine hundred miles away!"

Albrecht ran the few paces to the base of the palace wall and turned, crouching, with his hands clasped, palms upward, in front of him. Adolphus, following, placed a foot on Albrecht's hands, and was instantly catapulted up onto the highest point of the palace parapet. Here Adolphus, rearranging his glasses, peered into the distance.

"He's under a tree! Near Belgrade! There's a bottle beside him!"

"I hope he hasn't been at it!"

Albrecht threw a huge musket to Adolphus who caught it and quickly adjusted the sights.

"Wind speed?"

Gustavus wiggled his ears authoritatively.

"Three knots!"

Adolphus took aim and pulled the trigger. There was a massive explosion as a great bolt of flame shot from the barrel knocking Adolphus backwards onto the palace roof.


### 3

On the outskirts of Belgrade, Berthold was lying asleep under a tree. The exertion of a thousand-mile trip in under three minutes had induced an irresistible wave of fatigue, and he'd lain down for five winks which had got out of hand and turned into forty. The bottle of Tokay sat by his side. He had just begun to dream about one of the famous adventures of Baron Munchausen, when Adolphus's musket-ball struck the tree above him and dislodged an apple which fell onto his head. Berthold awoke with a start and, observing the apple, might have embarked upon a train of thought of Newtonian proportions had he not recalled his mission. He jumped up, grabbed the Tokay and, selflessly ignoring a call of nature, whizzed off South East.


### 4

In the harem, with only a few grains of sand in the hourglass left to fall, and with the executioner's assistant preparing the chopping block for me, the Sultan was bringing his opera to its close.

"If I have enemies who hate my guts,

I've no judge and court to try them.

I pop them into boiling oil,

And then I lightly fry them."

I charged in on Bucephalus, leaped to the ground, checked the hourglass against my own, and looked out of the window towards the horizon.

"If they forgive me, singing hymns,
I try pulling off their limbs,
How quickly they abandon when,
They haven't got a leg to stand on then."
To my dismay, I could see no sign of Berthold.
"I'm a modern man,
These days I find,
You have to be awfully cruel to be kind."
I turned form the window thinking that one of the benefits of being executed would be never to have to listen again to the Sultan's music.
"I'm a modern man,
You will agree,
It's either you or me."
The Sultan played the final excruciating chord of his opera, got up from the torturetron and examined the hourglass carefully.
"Well, time's nearly up, I think."
He raised his hand. The executioner's assistant guided me to the block and the blind executioner into a position where he stood a reasonable chance of decapitating me if he followed instructions. The Sultan, hand still raised, watched the last few particles of sand tumble through the neck of the hourglass. Sensing something, I twisted my head so that I could look out of the window. There, in the distance, I saw what could only be Berthold, etching his way across the landscape. As I opened my mouth to speak, the Sultan's arm dropped with awful finality, signaling the executioner's assistant to nudge the blind executioner into action. Something which promised something perhaps more awful than awful finality. The scimitar was in the middle of its downward arc as Berthold rocketed into the harem with his bottle and letter for me. The Sultan twitched the corner of his mouth and the executioner's assistant prodded the executioner who brought his blade to a halt touching my neck.

Peering at the hourglass, the Sultan and I agreed that Berthold had arrived with two grains of sand in my favor. The Sultan surveyed the new hole in the harem floor which Berthold had dug when coming to a halt. More builders. Berthold gave me the letter and the Tokay, then grabbed his weights and put them on.

"I'm not late, am I?"

I lifted my head from the block.

"No, no . . . not late."

My voice had a slight tremor. As I stood up, my pigtail, severed by the executioner, fell to the floor.

"I needed a trim."

I gave the bottle of Tokay to the Sultan who opened and tasted it without delay.

"Hmm. Delicious. You win."

The Sultan summoned his Treasurer.

"Allow my friend here to take from the treasury as much as the strongest man can carry."

So saying, he disappeared into his inner sanctum clutching the bottle of Tokay and as many of his forty-nine concubines as it was safe to have in one room at a time.

My companions and I followed the Treasurer down a long flight of subterranean steps to a massive iron door. This the Treasurer opened with a suitably massive golden key, admitting us to an enormous chamber filled with gold bars, chests of coins and piles of precious stones. We could hardly believe our eyes and almost forgot our routine line said in unison on awesome occasions:

"Cor, stack me, look at that!"

We now set about loading as much of the treasure as possible onto the powerful Albrecht. I smiled and rubbed the back of my neck. I recalled the Sultan's exact words: "As much as the strongest man can carry." He hadn't known about Albrecht. He soon would.

Leaving behind only one or two small items of inferior quality, the heavily laden Albrecht, followed by the rest of us,

staggered out of the treasury and up the stairs.

Not a happy man at the best of times, the Treasurer now looked decidedly gloomy. He hurried away to report to his master, wondering how he might make this sound like good news.

5

In the harem the Sultan was bathing, following a brief session of calisthenics with five of his more energetic odalisques. He had just poured himself more of my Tokay when the Treasurer bowled in with an uncharacteristic smile on his face.

"The Baron's taken all the treasure," he warbled. "You'd be surprised how big that room is when it's empty. May I suggest that it's just what Your Sublimity is looking for for the new torture suite."

The Sultan, never a man to waste words where action would do, snatched a sword from a guard and with one eloquent swipe cut off the Treasurer's head. Then clambering out of the bath and calling for his army, he raced from the harem. The Treasurer's head, lying where it had fallen in the lap of a terrified concubine, looked up at her and winked.

6

Mounted on Bucephalus, I led my party out of the palace and into the courtyard. Behind me came Albrecht, carrying seven eighths of the wealth of the known world, while Gustavus, Adolphus and Berthold brought up the rear. We planned to go to the quay side, borrow one of the Sultan's ships and set sail with the treasure before all hell let loose. However, before we had got halfway across the courtyard, a company of guards appeared and blocked our path. I nodded to Gustavus, who stepped forward, expanded his mighty chest with a deep intake of breath, and blew at the guards with such force that they were swept back across the courtyard and out through the main gate. Delighted, I congratulated Gustavus, but had scarcely finished doing so when the Sultan with more guards arrived behind us. Gustavus swung around, took another breath and repeated his first performance.

Now we set off again as quickly as Albrecht could walk. Meanwhile the Sultan, buried beneath a pile of guards, shouted a muffled order which was followed seconds later by a violent explosion. Suddenly we were showered with dust and debris. A second deafening explosion splintered the paving stones in front of Berthold. We spun around, searching frantically for the enemy. Then, there above us, we saw, gaping down at us from the palace parapet, the smoking mouths of the Sultan's mammoth cannon. Three more of these monsters spat fire, and we raced for cover as the walls surrounding the courtyard began to collapse.

## 7

A splinter of masonry landed on stage and bounced into the wings narrowly missing Bill and Desmond. A painted canvas cloud, its support ropes severed, swung down from the flies and sliced across the proscenium arch so close to the old man that its wind shook the feather in his hat. At the back of the auditorium the remaining boxes collapsed as exploding shells rocked the theater. The Sultan had begun another bombardment. The old man stepped across the footlights.

"And so . . ."

He tried to raise his voice above the noise.

"And so, as you can see, the Sultan is still after my head!"

The audience was fighting for the exit. The old man raised his arms.

"Don't go! Don't leave! I haven't finished!"

Light from the guttering candles threw his shadow into the auditorium where it seemed to embrace the audience. For a moment the fleeing crowd hesitated. He turned and appealed to Jeremy, Bill, Rupert and Desmond, who were standing, still dressed as the Baron's servants, petrified with fear in the middle of the disintegrating stage.

"Gustavus! Adolphus! Albrecht! We're about to make off with the Sultan's treasure! We can't just stop! Berthold!"

"The name's Desmond, mate! We're actors, not figments of your imagination!"

Desmond was at the end of his tether. He began to jump up and down.

"Get a grip!"

Another shell landed close by, breaking the remaining strands of the fragile spell. Once again the audience began to fight for the exit, while the actors ran from the stage.

Left on his own without an audience, the old man seemed to lose energy. He now looked even older.

"Come back! Come back!"

But his voice was very feeble and nobody heard him.

*"Sally's heart leaped into her throat."*

# PART IV

# THE BOMBARDMENT

*The Sultan ignores half-day closing. Jackson banishes the players. Sally gets cross. Death retreats. The Baron revives. More rubble. Sally gets crosser.*

## 1

ince the start of this bombardment, the Right Ordinary Horatio Jackson, though as keen as the next man to run for shelter, had made a great effort not to do so. In the first place, he didn't wish to be thought to have any overriding emotional response which might be considered to be inimical to scientific method. Secondly, logic dictated that in these circumstances, where one place was just as dangerous as another, you might as well stay where you were. And thirdly, there were so many generals and emissaries in the box that it was impossible to escape. The reason why there were so many generals and emissaries in the box was that they all wished to be seen doing the same as Jackson.

Jackson gathered up his papers with studied calm and spoke to Hardy. His voice gave evidence of cool intellectual control.

"What are the Turks playing at, it's Wednesday, isn't it?"

"Yes."

Hardy shook his head. It was indeed Wednesday, and, in the treaty drawn up two years previously, the Sultan had agreed that in the event of any future hostilities fighting on Wednesdays would definitely be out.

Seeing that most of the public had by now left the theater, Jackson deemed it logical to remove himself with haste. It was at this moment that a distraught Salt rushed across the wrecked stage.

"Sir, sir, I'm most terribly sorry about the show! I do hope . . ."

Jackson cut in, smiling pleasantly, glad to have something about which to demonstrate his lack of personal feelings.

"This theater is closed. You and your company must be out of the city by midday tomorrow."

"But sir . . . Please . . . No."

Salt began to search through his pockets.

"Please . . . Look at these highly favorable endorsements from every corner of Europe!"

As Jackson moved towards the exit at the rear of the box, Salt followed him, climbing in through the front. Pulling tattered papers from his pocket, he began to read, ten to the dozen.

"'Henry Salt and Son holds the mirror up to nature': *The London Clarion*. 'Mr. Salt's performance of Hamlet is wondrous to behold': *Paris Review*. 'A great night out': *Glasgow Herald*!"

Jackson and his entourage hurried away, pursued by the miserable Salt.

## 2

Sally, sitting in the wings, had been watching the Sultan's tale enthralled when the bombardment began. She was furious. How dare they? The old man who claimed to be Baron Munchausen was wonderful. With her eyes and mouth filled with dust she crawled to where she thought the center of the stage should be. The harem set had been completely ruined. The flats were broken and the canvasses holed. There was no going back. Had she been the small girl she sometimes pretended to be she might have cried. Everyone had disappeared. The old man

was nowhere to be seen. She was on her own. No sooner had this thought occurred to her when something touched her hair. She jerked her head back and found herself looking into the pale eyes of the old man's dog. She reached out to touch it, but it moved away, then stopped and whimpered, moved back towards her, then away again. This time Sally followed, crawling under piles of broken scenery and debris towards the back of the stage. Sally felt a surge of excitement. She had understood the dog. She caught up with it near the back of the stage. It was growling, hackles raised, at a tent of fallen roof beams and prop boxes. Peering into the dust Sally could just make out a dark shape. She couldn't quite see what it was doing. She inched her way forward past the growling dog. Suddenly the dust cleared. Sally's heart leaped into her throat. There, ten feet in front of her, kneeling on the body of the old man, was a thin, black figure with huge black wings. Lying on the floor, next to the old man's head, were a scythe and an hourglass. The hourglass sand was on the verge of running out. The winged figure had one skeletal hand on the old man's throat, while with the other it was extracting something bright and fluttering from his mouth. Suddenly, seeming to feel Sally's presence, the figure reared up and turned towards her, black wings spreading and hood falling back to reveal a mass of red hair erupting from a rotting, eyeless skull. The horrid thing moved towards Sally. She tried to scream. She thought she would faint. Grasping a heavy candlestick with its candle still burning she flung it as hard as she could at the advancing figure. Her aim was perfect, but the creature, on receiving the blow, changed into an image painted on a canvas backcloth and burst into flames. In seconds the canvas had become smoke and smoldering embers. Sally sat shaking beside it. After a moment the dog, wagging its tail, came and looked at her.

She crawled over to the old man. He looked very dead. Sick at heart, she pushed over the hourglass, preventing the last few grains of sand from running out. The old man opened his eyes. Sally spoke quietly for fear of killing him.

"Are you all right?"

"Am I dead?"

He sounded very feeble.

"No."

"Blast!"

This sounded more promising. But if he was going to die at any moment there was no time to be lost. There were questions to be answered.

"Who are you really?"

The old man groaned. Sally judged the irritating approach to be best.

"Baron Munchausen isn't real. He's only in stories."

"Go away . . . I'm trying to die!"

"Why?"

"Because . . . I am tired of the world . . . and the world is evidently tired of me."

"Why?"

No response. Sally prodded him ruthlessly.

"Why?"

"Why? Why? Why? . . . My audience has gone . . . It's all logic and reason now . . . Science! . . . Progress! . . . The laws of hydraulics, the laws of social dynamics, the laws of this that and the other! No place for three-legged cyclops in the South Seas . . . No place for cucumber trees . . . or oceans of wine . . . No place for me!"

The old man fell back exhausted. Sally pressed on.

"What happened in the story?"

"What?"

"In the Sultan's palace. Did you escape? Were you killed?"

"I don't know . . . It was all a very long time ago . . . Who cares?"

"I do."

Sally began to fear that she wasn't going to get her answers. The old man turned his head away.

"I'm very tired. Goodbye."

"Please tell me."

"No."

Sally began to think there was something childlike about the old man. These were the kinds of exchanges she normally had with younger people.

"Go on!"

"Buzz off!"

Now it was Sally's turn to get angry. She shouted at him.

"Tell me!"

The old man, surprised by Sally's vehemence, turned his head back and examined her face carefully. Sally felt uneasy. She hadn't really intended to shout. She knew this might spoil things.

"Please."

She tried to look deserving. He stared at her thoughtfully.

"You really want to know, don't you?"

He seemed surprised by the idea. The shape of his eyes changed slightly. He looked amused. Interested. For the first time since she'd found him here he smiled at her.

At this moment a shell whistled into the top of the theater and exploded with a thunderous bang, sending sections of wall crashing into the dressing room. A cluster of bricks bounced inches from the old man's head. Sally screamed and leaped to her feet.

"Stop it!"

More bricks descended from the flies in a column of dust. She shook her fists towards the roof.

"Stop it! We'll all be killed! And then I'll never know the end of the story!"

Another shell landed nearby. They seemed to be aiming for the theater. Sally had never felt so frustrated in her life before. With tears and dust in her eyes and ringing in her ears she clambered to the front of the stage, jumped into the auditorium and ran through the smashed stalls out into the burning town.

For a moment the old man didn't know that she'd gone. Then, levering himself onto his elbows he saw the slight figure jump from the stage and run towards the rear door.

"Hey! Where are you going?"

He struggled onto his knees.

"Come back! Take cover!"

But Sally had left the building. More shells landed nearby. The old man dragged himself to his feet with great difficulty and hobbled, stooping, to the front of the stage. He looked into the deserted auditorium mumbling to himself.

"Wretched child!"

Then, clambering awkwardly down from the stage, he shuffled off after her with the dog at his heels.

*"I was blown towards the waiting jaws of a whale . . ."*

*"It had been a long time since he'd gone in for this sort of caper."*

# PART V

# THE CANNONBALL

*Sally on the warpath. The Baron's eccentric mode of transport.*
*Death isn't quick enough. The Baron returns. Sally is convinced.*

## 1

hen Sally ran from the theater she knew precisely where she was going. She would climb onto the battlements and give the Sultan a piece of her mind. How dare he try and kill her new friend. Especially in the middle of his story. Her story. She was outraged.

Outside the theater she saw two incoming shells, their fuses burning brightly, shoot across the sky like comets. They looked pretty, but if they landed here they would put an end to her. She set off angrily towards the city wall.

The old man, whoever he was, was weird and funny and mysterious. He was the first grown-up person she'd met who made her feel that becoming a grown-up might be something to look forward to. Anybody who harmed or threatened him would have her to reckon with.

Crossing the square of the headless rider on his headless horse Sally once again passed beneath the gibbet. To the bodies hanging from earlier in the day had now been added the corpse of the wounded officer sentenced to death by Horatio Jackson.

## 2

On the battlements, facing the most concentrated source of enemy fire, a gun crew sat beside their mortar earnestly discussing the situation. Shells and cannonballs flew over their heads. Mike, a veteran of three campaigns, spoke first.

"Shouldn't we be firing back at them, sir?"

"No firing on Wednesdays, it's in the rules."

Don, the commander, who was unusual in having been a priest before becoming a soldier instead of the other way around, was a stickler for the regulations. Mike flinched as a shell whistled past.

"I know, sir, but ... "

"If we fire back at them, that's tantamount to saying that either we don't know it's Wednesday and are thoroughly confused, or we do know it's Wednesday but don't care."

Don stuck his fingers into his ears as Mike continued.

"But why are they doing it, sir?"

Tony, transferred to the gunners from the navy after his ship was sunk, and still smelling of rum, opened his eyes for the first time that day.

"Maybe they want us to think it's Tuesday or Thursday."

Don unplugged his ears.

"Eh?"

Mike repeated his question. Don replugged his ears.

"In my view they're trying to undermine our values—everything we stand for. Let us not forget, Wednesday has been half-day closing in this town since 1592. It's our tradition. 'Half-day closing—all day Wednesday.' If we let that go, it's the beginning of the end."

All three gunners retracted their heads beneath their shoulders as a cannonball whizzed across the wall and smashed into the town below.

A few yards from where the gun crew was crouching behind the battlement crenellations Sally arrived at the top of a long flight of stone steps. Here she stopped for a moment to survey the scene and regain her breath. In her billowing Sultan's Tale costume and with her pale face she appeared like a ghost.

Certainly an unlikely survivor of the brutal devastation all around. Seeing her, the gunners were on the point of deserting their post and running for it when a cannonball struck the battlements close by sending fragments of stone spinning through the air. The gunners ducked and clung together. Sally snatched up a handful of stone sherds and climbing between the crenellations began to fling them with all her strength towards the distant flashing mouths of the Sultan's artillery.

"Stop it! Stop it! We'll all be killed!"

The gunners looked at each other in astonishment. Mike checked the rabbit's-foot charm in his tunic pocket. Another cannonball hit the wall sending more stone splinters flying as the old man stumbled up the last few steps to the battlements. His ancient dog was with him, its tail firmly pressed between its legs. The old man saw Sally standing on the outer edge of the wall.

"Get down!"

He was so out of breath he could hardly speak. Sally set about gathering more missiles. The old man leaned heavily on his stick.

"You'll get us all killed!"

"I thought you wanted to die!"

Sally threw another stone. A smile flickered around the old man's eyes.

"Yes, but I'm old enough!"

Hearing the whine of an approaching shell he hurried forward, grabbed Sally and pushed her with the dog beneath the shelter of a cannon. The explosion was deafening and would no doubt have killed them all had not the old man acted promptly. When the dust cleared he took Sally by the hand and had begun to lead her to the top of the steps when he noticed the gun crew crouching abjectly behind their mortar. He frowned.

"Gentlemen, would it not be a good thing if you were to silence that enemy position?"

Mike and Tony shook their heads. Don removed his fingers from his ears.

"Eh?"

The old man repeated the question. Don spat against the wall.

"No, sir!"

"No?"

"It's Wednesday!"

The commander shouted with asperity. He replaced his fingers in his ears. The old man glowered at the gun crew in disbelief.

He said nothing but led Sally and the dog back to the shelter of the cannon. Leaving them there he returned to the gun crew where he picked up an ignition taper, held it in front of his face and thumped the side of his head with his fist. On the second blow sparks flew out of the old man's eyes and lit the taper. Sally and the gun crew watched, mesmerized. Now, with difficulty, the old man lifted a mortar shell and placed it in the mortar cannon. Then, holding the handle of the mortar with one hand he touched the ignition hole in the cannon with the burning taper. The commander was raising his hand to object when the mortar went off with a great explosion firing the shell and with it the old man who was still holding it out into the night towards the enemy camp. The gunners stared, open mouthed. Sally rushed forward to get a better view. The old man's dog, evidently having seen it all before, lay down under the cannon.

Meanwhile, several hundred feet above the plain, the Baron, for it was indeed he, was clinging to the speeding mortar shell wondering which would give out first, his fingers or his arm sockets. It had been a long time since he'd gone in for this sort of caper. Furthermore the mortar shell fuse was burning down in front of his face. One way or another there was bound to be a resolution to this situation fairly soon and he only hoped that it would be in his favor. He reflected that to have survived a career of impetuous follies for as long as he had must give rise to a certain optimism.

Looking down through the murk the Baron saw, to his

consternation, large-scale troop movements; soldiers, siege towers, ladders, battering rams, elephants and all the paraphernalia necessary for a major assault. The Sultan, under cover of darkness, was launching his attempt at a military victory.

The shell was now losing height and the Baron, spotting ahead what he took to be a Turkish gun emplacement, began to shift the position of his body to direct the flight of the shell at it.

As the Baron hurtled towards them, moments from impact, the Turkish gunners fired their cannon sending a massive grade 1 Saracen's Head type cast-iron ball thundering into the sky in the direction of the town. The Baron, judging that the moment had come to part company with the shell, let go and seized the Turkish cannonball as it sped past him. Seconds later he saw the flash and heard the explosion as his shell landed and destroyed the Turkish gun.

Whereas on the outward-bound journey the Baron had been able to hang on to the handle of the shell, the journey back was not nearly so easy, the cannonball being completely smooth. After nearly losing his hold a couple of times he managed to get on top of the projectile and sit astride it leaning forward into the wind and gripping it with his legs. Getting used to it he began to enjoy himself. This was almost like the old days. Perhaps there was life in the old carcass yet. It was with these thoughts in mind that he overtook what appeared to be another cannonball with a passenger on it. All this occurred so quickly that afterwards, reflecting on it, he wasn't sure whether it had happened or not. Out of the corner of his wind-swept eye the other passenger looked like a winged death. It seemed to turn and strike out at him with its scythe. He evaded the blow and sped on leaving the creature behind. The Baron's impression was that the winged death had been annoyed with him for having overtaken it. This thought gave him great pleasure.

He was in good spirits when, passing over the walls he

abandoned the cannonball, giving it a parting kick to send it harmlessly beyond the city, and sailed down onto the battlements holding his coattails out to slow his landing.

Ever since the old man's idiosyncratic departure, Sally had been staring hard into the sky scarcely daring to blink. Now she was convinced that he was Baron Munchausen. This was exactly what happened in one of the adventures and if it continued to form he should return any moment on a cannonball. Unless of course now that he was old he'd make a hash of it and get himself killed. The gunners certainly expected the old man's body to be lying at the foot of the walls. Don adjusted his chin strap.

"Stupid old git! What'd he do that for? He might have got us into a lot of trouble."

Mike tapped his temple.

"Don't worry, it didn't really happen."

"What are you suggesting?"

Don curled his lip. He'd had vegetarians in this unit before.

"Have you heard of this new thing called shell shock?"

Before Don could reply Tony leaped up.

"Look! Look! He's coming back!"

The gunners flinched as they heard the Baron's cannonball go over and then watched in stunned amazement as the Baron floated down to join them on the wall.

The Baron, feeling and looking ten years younger, was nevertheless not sufficiently agile to land without twisting his ankle and putting his back out. Sally helped him to his feet thrilled at being able to touch this eighth wonder of the world.

"You really are Baron Munchausen!"

The Baron didn't think that this was something he needed to be told. He turned to the gunners.

"The Turks are about to storm the walls."

The commander looked him up and down angrily.

"Who gave you permission to touch that mortar?"

The Baron was searching for a polite answer when a Turkish shell came whistling in and they all dived for cover. Following the explosion the Baron, Sally and the Baron's dog raised their heads to find that the gun crew and their gun had taken a direct hit and were no more. Sally took the Baron by the sleeve and led him down from the wall.

*"Please save us! Baron!"*

# PART VI

# THE BARON TO THE RESCUE

*Salt on the cusp. Sally's enthusiasm falls on deaf ears. The Baron reveals his pedantic side. Sally feels betrayed. The actresses stampede. The Baron's strange request.*

## 1

**S**alt, distraught and anxiously looking for Sally, lurched out of the main entrance to the theater. He was greeted in the street by a bolting horse dragging a broken carriage. The coachman's boots on the driving platform were all that remained of the horse's master. The back of the carriage was on fire. It was a harrowing sight. Salt reeled back into the theater foyer and slumped melodramatically against the door frame.

"That's it, it's the end, it's all over!"

The rest of the company, helping in the search for Sally, joined Salt and looked at each other in silence. They were tired and frightened. Salt continued to raise their morale.

"Generations of theatrical expertise snuffed out in the twinkling of an eye!"

He saw Sally and the Baron approaching the theater and rushed cautiously across the street.

"Sally!"

He pulled her away from the Baron.

"You stupid senile old windbag! Thanks to you we're to be thrown to the Turks!"

An explosion in the vicinity drove them into the theater. Sally glowed with excitement.

"He really is Baron Munchausen!"

Salt entered the auditorium where skips and boxes had been placed ready to be filled with costumes and props.

"He really is! The real one!"

"Oh shut up!"

In vexation Salt picked Sally up, dropping her into one of the skips and slammed down the lid. Sally pushed open the lid and stood up.

"But he is!"

Salt and the others began to pack, punishing Sally for having given them cause for concern by completely ignoring her.

"And he can save us!"

She turned to the Baron for support.

"Can't you?"

The Baron looked doubtful.

"Er..."

Having surprised even himself by his most recent exploit he was now drained of energy and not sure he could do anything other than sleep. Sally's mind was racing.

"I know! You could escape, find your amazing servants and bring them back to rescue us."

This was terrific. Everything she said sounded ridiculous. There was no way in which her father or anyone else in the company was going to believe this. And yet it was all true. They'd call her a liar and tell her to stop being stupid and then she, or rather the Baron, would tell them and if necessary show them that she wasn't either. She could hardly wait.

"He jumped onto a cannonball. He really did..."

She'd make it difficult for anyone to believe her even if they wanted to.

"... and flew away, miles into the sky, up above the elephants and soldiers and..."

Salt looked up. Sally knew he was going to call her a liar.

"Oh God, stop lying!"

This was delicious.

"I'm not lying."

She turned to the Baron triumphantly.

"Am I?"

The Baron sniffed and mumbled.

"As a matter of fact you are."

Sally faltered. What was he saying?

"But you did!"

Was he really going to betray her like all the other adults? Then she remembered that she wasn't entirely dependent for a history of events on the curiously unreliable Baron.

"Those soldiers on the wall saw it too!"

She recalled the final shell.

"Oh ... They were killed."

Salt groaned. Sally was cross.

"But he did!"

She looked daggers at the Baron who collapsed onto a bench.

"No I didn't."

Sally was incensed. Here she was again arguing with an older person younger than herself.

"Now you're lying!"

The Baron rubbed his back.

"I never lie."

Sally gripped the side of the skip enraged at the injustice of it all. Now that the Baron was lying everybody believed him, and even though they thought he was a stupid old fool they still preferred his word against hers. She burst into tears, climbed from the skip and ran backstage. The others, packing their belongings, looked at the Baron with hostility. He twirled his drooping moustache.

"I didn't fly 'miles.' It was more like a mile and a half. And I didn't actually 'fly,' I merely held onto a mortar shell in the first instance and then a cannonball on the way back."

"You maniac! You've done for us!"

Salt thought that of all the dangerous half-wits in the world it was just his luck to run into this one. He would gladly have given the old man a good shake if the dog hadn't growled at him. The Baron, however, had no intention of taking the blame.

"Actually, it makes little difference whether you're thrown out or remain here. The Turks are about to take the town."

Everyone stopped what they were doing and stared at the Baron in horror. Salt was the first to crack.

"And I'm just coming into my prime! Just on the cusp between Romeo and King Lear! My public will kill me for dying at a time like this!"

The floodgates having been opened, Violet, Rose and Daisy swept through. Violet threw herself at the Baron but was outmaneuvered by Daisy and Rose who elbowed her aside in a pincer movement. Daisy was clutching her habitual baby.

"Save us! Save us!"

Rose snatched the Baron's hand.

"Please save us! Baron!"

Violet thrust her way back into the fray.

"Baron! You are a Baron, aren't you?"

Daisy stuck the bewildered baby under the Baron's nose.

"You're our only hope!"

"Ladies, ladies, please, please!"

The Baron, at first flattered, now found himself in danger of being trampled underfoot. He took a deep breath, inhaling all manner of odoriferous airs emanating from the posse of actresses pressing towards him. He was overcome. He had in the past been unable to resist the entreaties of women and now, obviously, wasn't the time to begin.

"Ladies. I swear that as long as I, Hieronymus Carl Friedrich, Baron von Munchausen, live and breathe, you shall come to no harm."

"Oh yes, oh yes, say it again . . . "

Violet did one of the stage swoons for which she had once been famous.

"Ha!"

Salt was less easily impressed.

The Baron produced three red paper roses from inside his jacket and presented one each to Violet, Rose and Daisy.

"You so remind me of Catherine the Great, the Empress of all the Russias, whose hand in marriage I once had the honor to decline."

"They all remind you?"

Desmond thought this rather improbable.

"Yes, why not? Some bits here, some bits there!"

The Baron now addressed the whole company.

"I have a plan. I will set forth immediately . . . "

Here he drew his sword, got it stuck in the paneling above and behind him, freed it, but overbalanced and fell to his knees. He was put back on his feet by the ladies who might now have been forgiven for having doubts about the capabilities of their champion. The Baron continued unsteadily.

" . . . find my extraordinary servants, and with their help lift the siege and end the war."

He'd forgotten that this was Sally's idea. Salt threw his Richard III crown noisily into a box.

"Oh brilliant, very good, bravo!"

But everyone noticed that Salt was merely sarcastic and did not insist that the Baron leave the theater. Violet twiddled playfully with a button of the Baron's waistcoat.

"How?"

The Baron rescued the button.

"Ladies, I shall require your assistance."

He paused dramatically in expectation. No one knew how to put across his adventures better than he. The ladies chimed in on cue.

"Of course."

"Anything."

"Just tell us what to do."

The Baron fixed them with a masterful gaze.

"Kindly be so good as to remove your knickers."

*"He won't get far on hot air and fantasy."*

# PART VII

# THE BALLOON

*The odd balloon. Jackson deflated. The stowaway. The Baron explains his improbable plan. The storm.*

## 1

D uring the night, as the Sultan pushed home his attack on the walls, the Baron made an underwear balloon in the ruins of the theater.

Sally was astonished at the quantity of bloomers and camisoles gathered from the citizens and how quickly, under the Baron's supervision, they were all patched together. Everyone, from nearly the highest to the lowest, seemed to have contributed something, and although the Baron had a preference for the finest silk on account of its lightness he nevertheless insisted on using even the coarsest linen and calico rather than disappoint the donor.

A wooden frame was constructed for the mouth of the balloon, to which was attached Salt's galleon modified by the addition of a brazier. This would serve as the balloon's gondola.

From time to time Sally lent a hand, but she stayed clear of the Baron, with whom she was still extremely angry.

By dawn the work was nearly complete and the Baron had started to inflate the balloon by blowing hot air into it from braziers on the stage. Desmond and Bill were working the bellows. Neither of them had been exposed to quite so much ladies' underwear all at one time before and Desmond was feeling faint.

"Look at that. Isn't it beautiful? A dream come true. It's the dawning of the age of . . . lovely intimate things." Bill, disgusted with Desmond, watched the Baron watching the balloon slowly expand.

"It's madness! He'll kill himself!"

Desmond stopped pumping and fell into a trance.

"Yes, but well worth it, eh?"

The Baron snapped his fingers and waved them back to work.

Around the edge of the inflating balloon people were helping to loosen folds of material and encourage the hot air from the braziers to circulate within the envelope. Rupert, who was used to better things, and Jeremy the dwarf were lifting an expanse of none-too-clean underwear above their heads. Jeremy had gone without breakfast for fifteen weeks and four days.

"How do we know he isn't just saving his own skin, eh?"

Rupert moved away a couple of yards. Jeremy followed him.

"It's only because he's tall, isn't it?"

"Shut up!"

Rupert was tired of this theme. Jeremy punched at the silk slip.

"Let's face it, if he was a foot shorter this wouldn't be happening! And if he was two foot shorter his tales would be all about how he spent his life in fairy-land with other little people down some whimsical chocolate mine!"

Rupert picked Jeremy up and threw him into the billowing fabric.

Close to where the Baron was making final preparations to the galleon Violet was trying to poison Rose's mind.

"Can you really trust a man who makes balloons out of ladies' underwear?"

She snatched a pair of frilly bloomers out of Rose's hand. Rose snatched them back as the Baron turned and took them from her in exchange for a brilliant smile.

"Trust me, madam. Your underwear is in good hands."

Violet trod accidentally on Rose's foot.

The balloon now began to rise slowly from the stalls towards the hole in the roof. As it lifted it altered shape, the hot air pushing out its walls, so that the patchwork of pink and white undergarments became clearly visible.

While everyone's attention was focused on this remarkable sight, one of Horatio Jackson's generals who'd been observing the proceedings with interest slipped hurriedly away.

## 2

In the town hall, Jackson, Hardy and assorted generals and functionaries continued diligently to plan the war. They had been up all night and were exhausted, which gave them great satisfaction since they identified fatigue with self-sacrifice and achievement. The fact that they hadn't achieved anything was of little importance. Jackson pushed aside a pile of papers and maps.

"We need a simple plan. These are far too complicated. Simplicity is of the essence."

The generals and functionaries looked at one another in dismay. 'Simplicity,' 'essence,' more new words with which to come to terms.

At this point the general from the theater entered and went straight to Jackson.

"Sir, sir, those actors have made an air balloon. They're trying to escape!"

Jackson was overjoyed. Here was something to respond decisively to.

"Arrest them! Throw them out of the town!"

"We can't open the gates, sir."

"Well then, throw them over the walls!"

Jackson occasionally got the impression that some of his lectures in logic had fallen upon deaf ears.

"Yes, sir!"

The general exited. Jackson turned to Hardy.

"We can't start escaping at a time like this. What would

future generations think of us?"

Hardy nodded and shook his head wisely.

3

Back in the theater the balloon had reached sufficient height for the galleon, which was sitting on the forestage, to be swung down beneath it. The Baron gave the order and this was done. Then while the actors and citizens held guide ropes he stoked the brazier in the crow's nest. In a few minutes he would raise enough heat to begin his ascent.

Argus, the Baron's dog, stood in the prow of the galleon wagging his tail. Rose, having beaten back Violet and Daisy, climbed a ladder against the side of the galleon to give the Baron a farewell kiss. Those holding the guide ropes were now being lifted off the ground. Salt ran in from backstage with his customary fraught expression.

"Hey! You in the balloon! Have you seen Sally?"

"No! And the name's Munchausen! Baron Munchausen to you!"

The Baron, preoccupied with the balloon, had indeed not seen Sally for some considerable time. He gave the fire in the brazier another couple of blasts with the bellows and was climbing down the rigging to begin arranging his bags of ballast when Jackson's general charged into the auditorium with a platoon of soldiers.

"Stop! You're under arrest! Deflate that thing at once!"

The soldiers began to push their way through the crowd. Seeing them arrive, the Baron started to heave out bags of ballast as quickly as he could.

"Let her go! Let her go!"

Those holding the ropes released them immediately, allowing the balloon to rise gently, taking the galleon with it. The general was outraged.

"Shoot it down! Shoot the horrible thing down!"

He raised his saber.

"Take aim!"

The soldiers, squeezed together in the crowded auditorium, lifted their muskets awkwardly and took aim. The general had opened his mouth to give the order to fire when Argus launched himself from the galleon and landed with all four paws on the chest of the foremost soldier, knocking him backwards into his colleagues who toppled over in turn like dominoes, discharging their muskets harmlessly into the air.

As the balloon continued upwards unimpeded, the Baron addressed the audience below.

"Ladies and Gentlemen, I will return shortly with reinforcements. Don't lose heart. And to all the ladies to whom I am indebted for half a ton of frilly silk and lacy linen, don't catch cold. Au revoir."

The crowd cheered and Argus barked, jumping energetically up towards his master.

"Stay, Argus, stay! I'll soon be back!"

The Baron threw out the provisions he'd laid in for his dog as the balloon, rising steadily, cleared the top of the building.

4

The sound of distant cheering brought Jackson, Hardy and the other inmates of Jackson's office to the window. From here they saw the balloon with its gondola emerge from the top of the theater and float towards them above the square. The Baron caught sight of Jackson and doffed his hat to him as he passed over. Jackson wasn't pleased. He sneered contemptuously.

"He won't get far on hot air and fantasy."

Hardy nodded and shook his head in agreement.


5

The balloon was traveling steadily towards the perimeter wall, skimming roofs and chimney pots. The Baron, sorry at having had to leave Argus behind, accustomed himself to beginning this adventure on his own.

The first thing he set about doing was getting rid of the rest of the ballast. When passing over enemy-held territory he wanted to be high out of range of their gunfire. He worked quickly, levering bag after bag of heavy rubble out over the side of the galleon.

At the seventh or eighth bag the Baron realized instinctively that something was wrong. The bag didn't feel right, but he'd got a rhythm going and it wasn't until it was half over the side that he saw Sally's feet slide out of the neck. It was a great shock for him and he lunged at the bag clumsily, gripping it tightly but nearly letting its momentum carry him overboard.

For a second he thought he'd succeeded in saving her, but the next moment, which passed as an agonizing lifetime, he watched her slip from the sack and fall.

The Baron couldn't bear to look over the side. He slumped back, sickened, against the mast. Was there any point in going on? He thought not. Should he throw himself over the side and dash his brains out in the streets below? Almost certainly, yes. He wished that he could. In his youth he'd tried suicide on several occasions, but even his most determined attempts had ended in failure and been regarded as merely part of his adventures.

He was sunk in these miserable thoughts when he heard a

hard, high-pitched shout from somewhere below. Jumping to the side of the galleon he peered over. There, swinging back and forth about fifteen feet beneath the gondola, was Sally. The back of her dress was hooked on the galleon's anchor which was hanging on a length of rope. The Baron felt sick again. Her dress might easily tear or slip off the blunt anchor claw. His ancient nerves of steel felt decidedly brittle.

"Help!"

Sally knew that the Baron had seen her and was indignant that she should have to continue to shout for help. How many times did it take?

"Help!"

She waved her arms. The Baron nearly had a heart attack.

"Don't move! Don't struggle!"

"Help!"

"I am! Keep still!"

Slowly and very carefully the Baron, sweating, hauled up the anchor and Sally until he was able to grab hold of both of them. He pulled them into the galleon and collapsed onto the floor. Sally was shaking and wanted to scream.

"Thanks."

She sounded cool and unconcerned. This enraged the Baron.

"You've ruined everything!"

He kicked the mast and dented his boot.

"I'll have to douse the fire and put you down!"

He picked up a pail of water and moved towards the brazier. Sally pushed in front of him.

"I'm going with you!"

"You are not!"

The Baron tried to get past her. She clung to the rigging.

"I am!"

"No, you're not!"

"Yes, I am!"

Sally couldn't believe it. Here she was again arguing with one of Daisy's little brats. The Baron tried to control his temper.

"I absolutely and utterly refuse ... "

"If we go down now we'll land on the Turks!"

Sally pointed over the side, a smile of triumph on her face. The Baron looked down to see where they'd just crossed the battlements and were floating out over the Turkish camp. Below them the assault was in full swing with a fierce battle being fought along the walls. The Turks were attacking in strength and even Sally, with no experience of these things, could see that the situation for the town was desperate. She turned anxiously to the Baron.

"We've got to find your servants and get back here quickly!"

"That *is* what I had in mind!"

The Baron glared at her, raised his telescope to his eye and examined the crescent moon. Sally wasn't going to be intimidated. She smiled very sweetly.

"By the way. I forgive you for saying that I was lying the other day, about you flying on the cannonball, when I wasn't lying at all. So we can be friends again, can't we?"

The Baron's jaw dropped. He stared at her dumbfounded. She clambered over to him still maintaining the sweet smile.

"Where are we going?"

The Baron shook his head at her in disbelief and then nodded up ahead.

"To the moon."

"What?"

Sally didn't hesitate.

"That'll take ages!"

The Baron was impressed. She evidently continued to believe him.

"No it won't."

"Of course it will!"

"It won't!"

The Baron was exasperated. She evidently continued to believe him, selectively.

Sally wrinkled her nose. Being told you were going to the moon was one thing, being expected to believe that the journey could be accomplished in five minutes was quite another.

The Baron pursed his lips. Perhaps things would have been better if she hadn't snagged on the anchor.

Sally continued her inquisition.

"Why are we going there?"

The city and the Turkish camp were now almost out of sight. Far below was a river winding through forests. The Baron produced a pipe and proceeded to fill it.

"Because that's where I last saw Berthold."

He struck a match and sucked on the pipe.

"Have you ever been to the moon?"

"No."

Sally was guarded. She was suspicious of his avuncular tone. He blew a puff of smoke.

"Interesting place. The King and Queen are charming. You know about their detachable heads, don't you?"

"No."

"Ah, yes. Their heads go off for intellectual pursuits, leaving their bodies to get on with . . . more bodily activities. Unfortunately the heads and bodies don't always see eye to eye."

Sally nearly laughed, but didn't since she thought the Baron was now probably teasing her. She gave him what she hoped was a skeptical look. He struck another match.

"You do believe me, don't you?"

Sally responded cannily.

"I'm doing my best."

## 6

Sally didn't know how long they'd been in the air before they were engulfed by the tempest. It hit them suddenly and with terrific force, beginning with a blinding flash of lightning and a simultaneous crash of thunder as if they were at its core. A torrent of rain extinguished the brazier almost immediately and a violent wind tore at the balloon, shaking the galleon and swinging it in circles. The Baron and Sally clung to the rigging. Sally was terrified. She could hardly see or hear. Between ice-cold sheets of rain she caught glimpses of the Baron, his hat jammed over his ears, its feather beaten flat against the crown. She yelled into the wind.

"Are you scared?"

"Certainly not!"

The Baron tightened his grip on the ropes.

"Are you?"

"Certainly not!"

Sally didn't believe either of them.

That instant, a ball of lightning hit the balloon and ripped it, blazing, from the galleon, which began to fall, twisting and turning, until the rain became so dense that it was pushed upwards and then down as if riding waves at sea.

Sally had completely lost her bearings when, squinting through the wind, she saw above her the crescent moon, yellow and gigantic, stretching right across the firmament.

"...a gigantic disembodied head floated up
from behind one of the walls."

# PART VIII

# THE MOON

*The Baron gets younger. The King's head. Comfortable incarceration. The King's body. Uncomfortable incarceration. The Queen's head and body. The old man in the cage. Ariadne brings the key. Escape. The King's bed without the Queen's head. The demise of the three-headed griffin. The hair rope. Berthold is puzzled. Fall from the moon.*

## 1

rouching in the bottom of the galleon, Sally didn't see much for the rest of the journey.

When the storm eased she peered over the side to discover that they were indeed sailing on water. Though even while she watched the waves breaking around her they disappeared, draining away, leaving the galleon moving through what looked like sand.

Behind them, just above the horizon, Sally saw what she was sure was the earth. She turned to the Baron, who was asleep in the stern, and tapped his arm.

"We're here!"

The Baron opened a bleary eye and grunted. Sally scrutinized him closely.

"You look different—younger."

He got up.

"I've always been rejuvenated by a touch of adventure. But for heaven's sake don't you get any younger or I'll have to find a wet nurse."

Sally laughed out loud. Something she hadn't done for a long while.

Sailing on, they saw in front of them, in the distance, an

immense spherical structure. Getting closer they could see, inside, what appeared to be a small building. The Baron took the tiller and headed the galleon towards this.

"I've always been one of the king's favorites. We'll receive a right royal welcome."

Sally was wondering why the king of the moon lived in such a funny little place when, on passing into the interior of the vast sphere, she saw that what she had understood to be a small building was in fact the corner of a magnificent city full of grand and beautiful palaces. This was more like it.

This impression lasted until on entering the city itself, which seemed deserted, and sailing along one of its sand canals, Sally found that the beautiful palaces looked like dolls' houses. She was so confused by the changes in perspective and scale that for a moment she was convinced that if she reached out she could hold one of the palaces in her hand. She tried and failed.

And as if this weren't peculiar enough, while they advanced along the canal Sally began to hear music, a band playing, and cheering from what sounded like welcoming crowds. She looked around. There was no one in sight. She looked inquiringly at the Baron. He smiled and began to wave at the invisible multitude. Sally had a feeling he was only pretending to know what was going on.

The music and cheering had reached a crescendo when Sally and the Baron were nearly knocked off their feet as the galleon collided with something. Looking over the prow Sally was amazed to find that they'd hit a wall right in front of them, painted perspectively to look like a continuation of the canal. An examination of the buildings on either side showed that these too were paintings on flat two-dimensional surfaces. This was like being in the theater. Sally was on the point of trying to extract an explanation from the Baron when a section of wall swung closed behind them, effectively trapping them in a box. Sally was frightened, but she nearly jumped out of her skin

*" . . . a mass of red hair erupting from a rotting, eyeless skull."*

when a gigantic disembodied head floated up from behind one of the walls.

"Munchausen! At last!"

Taken by surprise, the Baron quickly recovered his composure.

"Your Majesty, what a pleasure to see you again."

He bowed deeply.

"May I introduce my friend, Sally. Sally, the king of the moon. Well, his head at any rate."

The king's refined and delicate features began twisting and contorting. He seemed to be in pain.

"I'm sorry, but I must insist on the correct title. Re di Tutto. The King of Everything. But you can call me Tutto. As a matter of fact the moon is a quite insignificant part of my domain."

The king, or to be precise, his head, reminded Sally of an Italian escapologist her father had once employed who was always going to jail. The Baron looked concerned as the king's face went into another spasm.

"My old friend, you seem to be in some discomfort. What ails you?"

The king's eyes rolled and crossed.

"Nothing ails me! Can't you see that by an effort of extraordinary intelligence and will power I am controlling and regulating the entire universe! Now I make spring!"

The king made a clucking noise like a chicken.

"You see! Spring!"

The Baron looked unconvinced.

"Hmm."

The king's aquiline nostrils dilated.

"I make spring and all you can say is 'Hmm'? Since you were last here, Munchausen, I, that is my head where the brilliant and important parts are located, have taken over all creation. Without my considerable mental power everything would be chaos. There'd be no stars, no planets, no life, no lunch, niente!

Not even you! 'Cogito ergo es,' I think therefore you is!"

Sally sneaked a look at the Baron and spoke without moving her lips like a ventriloquist.

"Your old friend's a lunatic."

The Baron replied in the same manner.

"So it would seem. He's certainly fallen prey to delusions of grandeur."

The king's face continued to twitch.

"Keeping my mind tuned to every molecule in the cosmos requires an enormous concentration, Munchausen, and having you on the loose doesn't help. You are to me like a mosquito in the Taj Mahal."

He made a sound like a mosquito.

"Your silly stories are a distraction!"

The Baron was stung.

"I beg to inform you, my liege, without my adventures you wouldn't be here!"

"So, I'm part of your 'adventures,' am I? Who's fallen prey to delusions of grandeur now? And next time don't whisper. It's rude!"

"Your Majesty, the truth is that my truth approximates more closely to the truth than your truth, and there's an end to it."

"We shall see!"

The king lowered his eyebrows and gave every indication of thinking hard.

In an instant the galleon vanished, together with the surrounding walls, and Sally and the Baron found themselves standing in a beautifully furnished, well-appointed drawing room. Well-appointed, that is, except that it was situated on top of a tall square pillar with a long sheer drop on all four sides.

Sally peered gingerly over the edge before moving quickly back onto the silk Persian carpet. The king's head hovered beside the top of the pillar.

"I'm sure you'll be very comfortable. As you can see I'm a

kind and civilized man."

Suddenly an expression of alarm knit the king's sensitive brow.

"Ugh! There goes my revolting body with the queen! Please don't look!"

Naturally Sally and the Baron looked, and following the direction of the king's horrified stare saw below, and at some distance from the pillar, a bulky headless body clutching at a woman who was trying to beat it off with a butterfly net. The king closed his eyes.

"You wouldn't believe my body and I are related. We're totally incompatible. It's so far down the food chain! So basic! So unmetaphysical! Ugh! When we're together it sticks its nasty fingers up my nose!"

As the king's head shuddered with disgust a hairy hand groped up from below, grabbed it, and pulled it down. The king's eyes opened wide with fear and loathing.

"Argh! No! Let me go! You brutish thing! How I despise you!"

The Baron and Sally looked cautiously over the edge of the pillar to where the king's body was trying to force the king's head back onto its neck. After a brief tussle the head was jammed in place and the body began stuffing food into it.

"Mangia! Mangia! Gimme Mangia!"

The reassembled king belched loudly.

"I can't eat without a mouth and I need to eat to do all the other beastly things!"

He farted and laughed.

"Yahoo! I'm back in business!"

The body thumped the head with its fist.

"Pretentious, namby pamby head!"

It stuck its fingers up the head's nose just as the head had said it did.

Sally was astonished at the transformation. The king's voice had become deep and gruff and his face now looked quite different, rounder and heavier. Not to mention his appallingly crude behavior. She decided she disliked him even more with his body than without.

The Baron, embarrassed on behalf of the queen, attempted to divert her. He raised his hat and bowed with a flourish.

"Your most wondrous Highness!"

"Right! Baron!"

The reunited king, food dripping all down his front, elbowed the queen aside.

"The real truth of the matter is the last time you were here you tried to make off with my queen! So this is for you! A nasty place to rot in!"

Once again Sally and the Baron's surroundings suddenly changed. The elegant drawing room disappeared and was replaced by a small straw-filled cage suspended in space. The king roared with laughter.

"I'm sure you'll be very uncomfortable. As you can see I'm a cruel and uncivilized man."

At this point the head escaped, spitting out food as it spiralled up away from the body.

"Yuk! You can't even keep hold of me, you dolt!"

Now the body ran blindly to and fro throwing food and anything else it could lay its hands on at where it supposed the head to be. The head was jubilant.

"Troglodite! I'm trying to concentrate on higher things! Go and amuse yourself in the slime!"

Here, the queen, having sneaked up under the head, caught it in her butterfly net. It went berserk, thrashing about in the net.

"No, no let me go! I've got tides to regulate! Comets to direct! I haven't got time for bodily functions! Not even the quiet ones!"

The queen and the king's body ran off with the king's head

in the net.

Sally watched them go and felt a very long way from home. She had begun again to worry about her father and the rest of the theater company and the more she thought about them the angrier she became with the Baron. She rounded on him.

"One of the king's favorites?"

The Baron sat down at the edge of the cage and tried to make himself comfortable.

"I can't understand it."

"He said the last time you were here you tried to make off with his queen. Doesn't that ring a bell?"

Sally put her hands on her hips and stuck her elbows out the way Rose did when she was angry.

"It's quite untrue!"

The Baron's denial was perhaps a little too forceful. He checked himself.

"I er . . . I was merely polite to her."

Sally shook the cage bars. The Baron took out his pipe.

"I'm afraid the 'King of Everything' has little regard for the facts. Let this be a warning to you."

Sally was in no mood to take lessons from the Baron.

"What do you mean?"

"This is the fate of those who ignore the truth."

"What is?"

"To end up . . . "

Sally cut in accusingly.

"In a cage on the moon?"

The Baron struck a match.

"This cage isn't real. It's just part of the king's lunacy."

Sally kicked a bar which rang with a dull rattle.

"Solid enough."

"I see we're not in a very helpful frame of mind."

The Baron was getting tetchy. He bit too hard on his pipe and snapped the clay stem. Sally didn't offer sympathy.

"How are we supposed to save the town from here?"

The Baron barked back.

"The town's perfectly all right! The assault's over! Everyone's safe!"

"How do you know?"

"I just know."

## 2

Meanwhile, back at the siege, the Turks were swarming up ladders onto the battlements where the town's soldiers and citizens engaged them in ferocious hand-to-hand fighting. Things looked bad.

## 3

Sally, unconvinced by the Baron's reassurances, scowled at him and set about examining the cage. There wasn't much to examine. It was round, made of metal, there was a locked door on one side and an area at the bottom covered with straw. After two minutes she felt she knew all she wished to know about it and more. She jumped onto the straw and then off again rapidly as she heard a voice from underneath.

"Ow!"

The Baron leaped up.

"Come out! Come out of there!"

He drew his sword and poked it into the straw.

"Ow! Stop that!"

An indignant old man stuck his head out of the straw.

"What'd you do that for?"

"I'm sorry, I thought you might be unfriendly."

The Baron sheathed his sword.

"Of course I'm unfriendly! You'd be unfriendly if I prodded you!"

Sally stared at the old man. She had a sense of having met him somewhere before.

"Who are you?"

The old man thought for a moment.

"I've forgotten. I've been here so long."

Sally was upset. She turned to the Baron.

"We'll be like that if we don't escape!"

"Why are you here?"

The Baron spoke calmly. The old man thought again.

"I'm a very wicked criminal."

Sally was intrigued.

"What have you done?"

Sally's eyes narrowed. Was he teasing her?

"Well, for one thing I'm in here. And for another ... "

The old man struggled to his feet.

" ... I've got these shackles on!"

He shuffled out of the straw dragging two heavy weights, one attached to each ankle.

"Berthold!"

The Baron was ecstatic.

"Eh?"

The old man looked puzzled.

"It's Berthold!"

The Baron grinned at Sally and embraced Berthold, for it was indeed he.

Sally now realized why she thought she'd met him before.

It was uncanny. He looked just like Desmond. Or at least very much like Desmond's portrayal of Berthold.

The Baron was shaking Berthold.

"Berthold! It's me! The Baron! I knew I'd find you on the moon! We're taking you back to earth to help us fight the Sultan!"

Berthold didn't seem in the least bit pleased to see the Baron and tried to push him away.

"Get off! Get off me!"

"You're Berthold! Berthold, my old servant and comrade! Those leg irons are to slow you down! Stop you tearing off all over the place!"

Berthold looked askance at the Baron.

"You must be joking."

"You always wore them! Remember?"

Berthold broke away from the Baron.

"You're crackers!"

"I'm Baron Munchausen."

"That sounds nasty. Is it contagious?"

Sally butted in.

"We're wasting time."

She was dejected. Berthold didn't bear much resemblance to the Berthold in the Sultan's Tale. Then he'd been young and fit. Now he was old, feeble and had lost his memory. And as if that weren't bad enough, he too was a prisoner. There didn't seem to be much hope. At that moment a shadow fell across the cage making Sally jump. She spun around and saw the queen's head hovering close to the bars. The Baron had seen it too.

"Ariadne!"

"Darling Baron!"

Ariadne was holding something between her teeth which made her difficult to understand.

"I'm sorry I couldn't speak to you before, but Roger's so difficult. I think he's having some sort of identity crisis."

She now inserted the object she was holding between her teeth into the door and Sally saw that it was a key and that she was going to release them. Ariadne turned the key in the lock by rotating her head three hundred and sixty degrees.

"Dear Baron, you're much too handsome to languish in a cage."

She pulled the door open, let go of the key and smiled seductively. The Baron scanned the surrounding space. He spoke nonchalantly.

"Where exactly is Roger?"

Ariadne made a strange high-pitched whinnying noise which startled everyone.

"Ohohooo! He's in bed with my body!"

Her eyes rolled upwards showing the whites.

"Oooh! Stop it! But if he discovers that my head's with you . . . Aaah! Quickly, climb into my hair! Oooooaaah!"

She placed the side of her enormous head with its coils of hair against the open cage door.

Sally thought that there were altogether too many things which she didn't understand. She whispered to the Baron.

"Why is she making those funny noises?"

The Baron seemed embarrassed and looked at Berthold, who looked the other way. Sally was annoyed. Whenever two or more adults were gathered together there were always secrets. She stuck her hands on her hips again. The Baron could see that he was going to have to say something. He twirled his moustache.

"Her body's with the king . . . and he's tickling her feet."

He turned quickly to Berthold.

"Berthold!"

He took him by the arm and pulled him out of the straw.

"Come on!"

Berthold struggled.

"Let go of me!"

"You're coming with us."

"No chance."

The Baron was astonished.

"Why not?"

Berthold concentrated.

"Can't remember."

The Baron stepped back.

"That's it!"

The Baron waved to Sally.

"Help me."

Between them they dragged the reluctant Berthold, weights and all, out of the cage and onto Ariadne's head where they all clung precariously to her hair and ornate headdress. Ariadne's head then sped away across what appeared to be the surface of the moon uttering strange squeaks and moans and little laughs as it went.

Sally was interested to note that this part of the moon was covered with odd-looking constructions. Brick and stone edifices, huge temples and palaces, marble towers and rotundas, none of which seemed to have been completed.

She conjectured that things probably never got finished here because of the constant battles between heads and bodies. She didn't ask the Baron in case he knew and it pleased him.

Ariadne's head lurched to an abrupt halt in the shadow of one of these unfinished structures.

"Ooooh! Ahh! Mmmmmm! Oh, Baron, I must get back to Roger before he notices I'm headless!"

"I quite understand!"

The Baron climbed down from the queen's head and helped Sally and Berthold after him. Ariadne's head swiveled around and hovered up close to the Baron, her eyebrows undulating passionately.

"Darling, take me with you."

"My dear . . . "

The Baron was momentarily staggered.

" . . . back to earth?"

"Yes!"

"Er . . . without your body?"

Ariadne pouted.

"I thought you loved me for myself!"

"Oh I did, I mean, I do. Of course I do. It's just that . . . "

Sally interrupted. She was getting tired of this.

"We've got to go!"

Ariadne's head seemed to calm down.

"No, you're right, it's impossible. It was just a mad thought. Here, take a lock of my hair."

She spun around and the Baron drew his sword and cut a large plait of hair from behind her left ear. Berthold, who suspected he was going to have to carry this, protested.

"Just a lock, cocky! Not the whole carpet!"

The Baron put his sword back in its scabbard, slung the length of hair around Berthold's neck, and bowed profoundly.

"I shall treasure it always."

Ariadne blushed and began to make weird noises again.

"Ooooooh! Aaaaaaah! The king's . . . Haaaa! I must go! Oohohoho! Au revoir, dear Baron! Oooooeeeaaah! Good luck! Aaaaaaaah!"

The Baron plucked a red paper rose from inside his jacket and placed it between Ariadne's teeth, whereupon she shot quickly away across the moonscape.

"Ahhhahaha! I'm on my way, Roger! I'm coming!"

Sally was glad to see the back of her.

## 4

While the queen's head was setting free the Baron, Sally and Berthold, her body was in bed with the once-more complete king, who was tickling her feet.

"Ticky, ticky, ticky . . . "

He played with her toes.

"This little piggy went to market, this little piggy stayed at home, this little piggy . . . "

The bed was vast, with great sweeping baroque volutes for

its headboard and legs. The giant occupants took up only a small corner of the mattress.

The queen's body, with the exception of her feet, was under the bed covers and the king was so engrossed in trying to make her laugh that he was unaware that her head was absent.

"Hey, hey! I'm coming to get you! I'm going to give you a big bacio!"

He began to tickle his way under the bedclothes to where her head should have been.

"Here we go, darling! Ticky, ticky, ticky!"

Halfway up her body the king noticed, for the first time, the lack of any audible response.

"Hey, you're very quiet today, eh? Why is that? You not feeling good? Don't tell me you have another headache? Come on, I give you a big bacio and make it better."

He continued up the bed to the pillow and threw back the covers.

"My God! You've got no head! No wonder you're so silent! I guess at least you can't have a headache if you ain't got no head! Where is it? Maybe I'm too rough and knock it off, eh?"

He began rummaging in the bedclothes.

"Hey, we can play head and seek! Yoo-hoo! Where are you? I'm going to find you!"

Suddenly the truth dawned on him.

"It's with the Baron! I'll kill him! That little . . . ! piccolo . . . ! And you said size didn't matter!"

The king was now in a terrible fury. He stood up and bounced on the bed.

"Fetch me my radish club and celery sword!"

He hesitated.

"Oh, they're out of season. OK. OK. Bring the asparagus spear! The deadliest vegetable in my arsenal! I'll fix that midget Baron!"

He paused for a moment and listened. Silence.

"Fine, fine, I'll get it myself! Who am I kidding! Not only are there no servants here, but they're all totally incompetent!"

He climbed off the bed.

"Sybil! Sybil! Feeding time! Pranzo! Dinner!"

Seconds later a giant taloned claw ripped through the paneling of the bedroom door. The king dodged a flying wood splinter.

"Mind the paintwork! You clumsy brute!"

## 5

Sally and Berthold plodded behind the Baron, who was leading them towards the distant tip of the moon's crescent. The sand was soft, which made the going tiring, and Berthold kept falling behind.

As they skirted a mysterious saucer-like structure, they heard a weird shrill squawking sound coming from the direction of the royal palace. Looking back they saw a tiny speck above the horizon zig-zagging towards them. The Baron was out of breath.

"It's the king on his griffin! Come on! Faster!"

He set off again.

"We can't. Berthold can hardly move!"

Sally was frantic. She'd only just begun to believe that they'd really escaped from the cage. The Baron waved his arms impatiently.

"Take his weights off!"

"I have!"

"What?"

How was it, Sally wondered, that the Baron was so brilliant and dim at the same time?

"He can't run any more! He's old!"

This was obvious, wasn't it?

"Nonsense. He's just out of practice!"

Sally would have stamped her foot if she'd been on something more solid than sand. She glanced back at the griffin, which was now no longer a speck but a recognizable griffin of the three-headed variety with a mammoth wingspan. The king could be seen sitting astride it holding the three pairs of reins in one hand and a spear in the other. The heads squawked horribly.

"It's going to catch us!"

Sally, the Baron and Berthold began running again as fast as they could.

Gaining on them fast, the king, his head securely strapped to his body, raised his asparagus spear and flung it hard at the puny figures below.

Berthold, who'd once more fallen behind, heard the rush of air from the asparagus spear as it whizzed down at them. He looked over his shoulder in panic.

At that moment the spear thumped, quivering, into the ground and Berthold ran straight into it, knocking himself out. Sally and the Baron ran back to help him as the griffin arrived overhead and began circling noisily.

The king had never been particularly fond of the griffin which was mechanical and needed oiling, and the griffin had never been very fond of the king who was negligent and let it rust. Now the king was having difficulty in controlling its three heads which bickered and fought continually amongst themselves, about nothing at all as far as he could see. He was tugging ineffectually at the reins when it occurred to him how he might achieve a temporary peace and unity of purpose in the ranks. He leaned forward in the saddle and shouted at the starboard head.

"You can have the tall one with the hat, because you're my favorite!"

Then to the middle head.

"You can have the old bald dead one, because you're my favorite!"

And finally to the port head.

"You can have the little girl because you're my favorite."

This, to the king's satisfaction, did indeed seem to pacify the heads, but no sooner had he settled back in the saddle than they got excited about their preferential gifts and went into a sickening dive.

On the ground the Baron and Sally were trying to revive Berthold. The Baron looked up as the griffin began its dive, and with enormous prescience and presence of mind instructed Sally to run away from Berthold in the opposite direction to himself.

This they did.

As soon as the king saw the Baron's tactics he knew he was in trouble. The griffin rarely listened to him at the best of times and getting it to change its minds in the present circumstances wasn't going to be easy. He hauled back hard on the reins.

"Whoa! Whoa! Up! Up! Together! Together!"

The two outer heads were now straining in opposite directions, one pulling towards the Baron, the other towards Sally, while the center head followed a vertical line towards Berthold. The greater the distance the Baron and Sally put between each other, and the closer the griffin got to the ground, the more obtuse became the angle between the outer necks. The king could now be plainly heard screaming desperately.

"Teamwork! Teamwork! Pull up! You're the last of your species!"

Unable to cope with the strain any longer, the griffin, only a hundred feet from the ground and plummeting fast, split into three.

Sally and the Baron threw themselves flat as great cogwheels, springs and feathers rained down on them.

On impact, the king's body was buried deep in the sand while his head broke free and ricocheted off into outer space.

"Free! Free! At last! The body's dead! Now I can concentrate on my great task! Pure thought!"

The head was receding fast.

"Thank God, no more body! Who needs it?"

Sally watched it go.

"Oh no! Oh No! I got an itch! I got an itch!"

She heard a sneeze as it disappeared out of sight.

Sally trudged back towards Berthold wondering how much more excitement she would have to cope with before getting something to eat. She looked at the Baron as he stomped back through the sand. He certainly seemed to be lucky. So far.

When they reached Berthold he was regaining consciousness. He opened his eyes and saw the Baron.

"Baron! Baron Munchausen!"

Bashing his head against the asparagus spear had evidently restored his memory. He got up and threw his arms around the Baron.

"Baron! Baron! It's so good to see you!"

"Let go! Get off me!"

The Baron endeavored to disentangle himself.

"We've been through all this already!"

He pushed Berthold away.

"I'm Berthold! Berthold! Your old servant and comrade! Remember?"

"Yes!"

The Baron straightened his collar irritably. Berthold gazed around.

"Where are we?"

Sally emptied the sand from her shoes.

"On the moon."

She managed to sound quite casual about it.

"Oh yeh? Same old Baron, eh?"

Berthold winked at her. Conveying the impression that he didn't believe a word of this either. Sally's sense of urgency returned.

"Can we go now?"

The Baron gave her some strands of
Ariadne's hair.

"Get weaving!"

He set off. Following his example Sally
began to weave the hair into a rope. They'd
only gone a few yards when Berthold called a
halt. He seemed cross.

"Hang on, hang on! It's all coming back!
I've been stuck here for over twenty years,
since the last time you were on the moon!
You abandoned me here! You swine! You
toddled off with the queen of tarts and left me
to rot in that parrot cage, didn't you? And
now you come back here, when it suits you,
having wasted half my life, and expect me to follow you to the
ends of the earth!"

The Baron twirled his moustache.

"Yes."

"Oh, all right."

And to Sally's amazement the Baron and Berthold moved off
again perfectly amicably.

The Baron led the way towards the sharp point of the
crescent moon. He was obviously an expert at hair weaving and
Sally wondered where and how he'd got his practice.

Berthold appeared to have completely recovered from both
his knock on the head and twenty years in the parrot cage,
though he was still very slow, even without his weights.

Sally had lost all sense of time. She knew that she should get
back to earth and the town as quickly as possible, but she had no
idea whether she'd been away for a month or a minute.

Soon their path began to narrow rapidly, until nearing the
point of the crescent Sally feared that they'd fall off one side or
the other. Unable to go any further the Baron spliced the various
lengths of hair-rope together, tied a loop in one end and threw it

over the tip.

Sally's mind was teeming with questions to which she knew she wouldn't get any satisfactory answers. The Baron turned to her as if reading her thoughts.

"This is precisely the sort of thing that nobody ever believes!"

He dropped the rest of the rope into the abyss.

"Berthold, you go first. Then you, Sally."

Berthold squeezed past them, stretched forward and grabbed hold of the hair rope. He was obviously scared half out of his wits. Sally watched nervously as he closed his eyes and fell away clinging tenaciously to the thin auburn plait. Sally couldn't decide whether she thought he was a game old bird or an idiot.

Now it was her turn. She closed her eyes and followed Berthold. It was worse than she'd imagined. The rope spun around, making her giddy, it was difficult to grip, it hurt her hands, and there wasn't enough of it. Below her was Berthold's shiny bald pate, above her the soles of the Baron's boots. The Baron, for some reason unknown to Sally, remained confident.

"Berthold! Do you know where the rest of the gang are?"

"Not a clue."

Sally thought that Berthold, while being rather nice, probably wasn't going to be much help. She slid down the rope after him. Predictably, to Sally, Berthold soon reached the end of the rope, although this seemed to come as a surprise to Berthold.

"That's it! Finito! There's no more rope! Mind out! I'm coming back up!"

Sally didn't think it possible for Berthold to climb back up again. Even if he had the strength, which she doubted, she certainly didn't and she was in the way. The Baron called down from above.

"Wait a moment."

He let down a length of hair rope.

"Here, tie this to the bottom."

Sally fed the rope down to Berthold, who examined it

carefully.

"Where'd you get this from?"

He waved it at the Baron.

"From the top."

"From the top?"

Sally observed Berthold's perplexed expression spread from his face across the top of his bald head.

"Naturally."

The Baron sounded exaggeratedly patient.

"Where else would I get it from?"

"But . . . "

"Yes, yes, yes. Hurry up and splice it to the bottom so that we may continue our descent!"

Berthold began to splice the rope. He was clearly deeply impressed by the Baron's explanation.

"Oh, very clever. Great. Why didn't I think of that?"

He grinned broadly at Sally. He was proud of the fact that his teeth were his own.

"That's why he's a Baron and I'm a prole."

This was the moment at which the hair rope, for whatever reason, ceased to do its job and Berthold, Sally and the Baron pitched helplessly into space.

## 6

The fall wasn't unpleasant. At the beginning Sally was miserable.

"We'll never rescue them now, will we?"

But after that she'd seen the earth increasing in size below them and realized that they were indeed falling and not merely tumbling aimlessly in space where they were likely to meet the tiresome king's head, and she felt a little happier.

Looking down she could see what she took to be great green and brown continents surrounded by blue sea and covered with whirlpools of white cloud. Very soon she could make out rivers, lakes and mountains. The trio seemed to be gathering speed. Berthold began to look increasingly apprehensive.

"It's thirty-two feet per second per second! Know what I mean?"

"Oh shut up! Have a bit of faith!"

Sally wasn't much reassured by the Baron's carefree attitude. She'd become aware of the fact that, although grown up, he was just as capable of showing off to her as she was of showing off to him. He waved at her and pointed below.

"Look! A volcano! Mount Etna, I'd say!"

Following the direction of the Baron's outstretched arm Sally saw a mountain with a hole in the top of it from which smoke was pouring. She'd heard about volcanoes. Now she was heading straight into one.

*"Can I help you tiny mortals?"*

# PART IX

# THE VOLCANO

*More giants? Vulcan and the Cyclopes. Mrs. Vulcan. Tea is served. The waltz. The Baron succumbs. Sally gets impatient. Vulcan blows his top. Good-bye to Etna.*

## 1

nside the volcano of Mount Etna there was considerable turbulence, but not of the kind anticipated by Sally.

It was here that for centuries Vulcan, blacksmith and armorer, by appointment to the gods, had worked at his forge making faultless swords, shields, latterly cannon, and all kinds of weapons of war.

As business had boomed over the millennia Vulcan had employed Cyclopes to help him keep up with the orders. These one-eyed assistants were excellent at their jobs and for the greater part of eternity worked together in harmony with Vulcan. The exception to this was the occasion, every hundred years, when contracts came up for renewal.

Vulcan, who was in all other respects a model employer, had an aversion to parting with money, and these negotiations always made him irritable.

Now he was confronting the Cyclopes who had downed tools, turned off most of their furnaces and were threatening a go-slow. He stood in the middle of the great cavernous workshop, a tough muscular man wrapped in a leather apron, picking up lumps of burning coal in his bare hands and hurling them at the Cyclopes.

"Two and a half percent on the basic rate is my final offer!"

A Cyclops swung his shovel and returned the blazing coal back towards Vulcan. The Cyclopes were shouting and waving their hammers.

"Five percent on the basic rate!"

"Six percent!"

"And a separate agreement for overtime!"

"No deal without an agreement on early retirement!"

"Five percent or no increased production!"

Vulcan slung another red hot coal at them.

"Two and a half percent! Take it or leave it!"

It was in the course of this fight that the Baron, Sally and Berthold plunged into the mouth of the volcano and came to an abrupt halt, landing, luckily, in a pit of powdery fluorspar used to raise the temperature in the iron ore smelters.

Vulcan and the Cyclopes stopped fighting and looked in surprise at the cloud of dust rising from the other end of the workshop. Picking up a short-sword, Vulcan led the way, stealthily, towards it.

Sally, the Baron and Berthold lay, mildly stunned, at the bottom of the fluorspar pit. Sally was the first to open her eyes.

"I'm still in one piece . . . I think."

She lifted an arm and moved a leg exploratively. The Baron got up and began beating the dust out of his hat.

"I can't imagine why. Our descent into what I assume to be Mount Etna should have been slowed by a rising cushion of warm air, but the damned thing would appear to have gone out."

Sally was trying to make up her mind about what she thought of the Baron complaining in these circumstances when Berthold, who'd crawled to the rim of the pit, struck fear into her.

"Oh no! . . . Not more giants!"

Sally and the Baron scrambled up to join him.

Looking along the length of the cathedral-like workshop,

they saw Vulcan and the Cyclopes, heavily armed, advancing towards them. Berthold gulped, loudly.

"I've got nothing against giants, personally. Some of my best friends are giants . . . "

The strange one-eyed mob was getting closer. Berthold slid back down to the bottom of the hole and cringed.

"If only they weren't so big!"

Vulcan, followed by the Cyclopes, reached the edge of the pit. They seemed to Sally to be even bigger than the king and queen of the moon. They were certainly more threatening. Vulcan ran his fingers along the sides of his perfectly tempered steel blade.

"Can I help you tiny mortals?"

"I sincerely hope so."

The Baron began to climb out of the hold. Sally was impressed by his bravery. However, to her amazement, when he reached Vulcan and stood up straight, it became apparent that he was at least six inches taller. She looked at Berthold in disgust and helped him up to join the Baron.

"I am Baron Munchausen. You may have heard of me."

Vulcan looked blank. He seemed displeased to have discovered that he was shorter than the Baron.

"My friends and I are looking for three men. One with exceptional eyesight, one with superb hearing and powerful lungs, and one who's extremely large and strong."

Vulcan bridled.

"We're all extremely large and strong here! I'm Vulcan the God, and these are my giant employees, the Cyclopes."

He turned and shouted at them savagely.

"Who are, even now, going back to work!"

The Cyclopes looked at each other and muttered.

"That's it! Go slow! Go slow!"

"Go slow!"

"Go slow!"

Then they all moved away in slow motion, leaving Vulcan

tugging at his beard.

Sally sneaked a closer look at him. He was strongly built, hairy, covered with grime and with large bulbous eyeballs. He looked quite deranged. Sally liked him immediately. He reminded her of one of her father's actors, in her opinion the best, who got blind drunk occasionally. Her father then punished him by not giving him good parts. Vulcan beckoned to them.

"I'll give you a tour."

The Baron, Sally and Berthold followed Vulcan around his vast workshop. He showed them huge steam hammers, enormous iron smelters and furnaces, and great quantities of arms, including exquisitely made muskets, pistols and cannon of all descriptions. Sally was reminded of the cannon being used in the siege and thought how vile they were in spite of sometimes being beautifully cast or engraved. Vulcan caught her eye.

"I'll supply arms and equipment to anyone who's prepared to pay the price. Greeks, Trojans, Romans, Huns . . . It's not my problem if they're daft enough to slaughter each other."

At this point, Vulcan, irritated beyond endurance by the go-slowing Cyclopes, thumped one.

"You manky crew!"

The Cyclops lifted his twenty-pound hammer as if to retaliate, but turned away spitting and cursing. Vulcan stuck his chin out and bellowed after him.

"Go slows don't impress me! I'm a God! I've got all the time in the universe!"

The Cyclopes now went so slowly that some of them fell over. Vulcan thrust his hands into his apron pocket and moved on.

"I hate them! In the old days the staff got their wages, on the dot, every thousand years. This lot expects it every century. It's outrageous!"

They were passing a large, long cylindrical object with a pointed end. The Baron stopped to look at it.

"What is that, may I ask?"

Vulcan smiled and scratched his beard.

"This is our prototype 3X Peacemaker, intercontinental, radar-sneaky, multi-war headed nuclear missile."

"Ah."

The Baron twirled his moustache.

"What does it do?"

"Kills the enemy."

Vulcan seemed to be enjoying himself. The Baron couldn't resist catching him out.

"*All* the enemy?"

Vulcan didn't hesitate.

"*All* the enemy. And all their wives and all their children and all their sheep and cattle and cats and dogs. All of them. All gone for good."

He smiled and did a funny little skip. Sally wasn't amused.

"That's horrible."

Vulcan looked at her wide-eyed like a parody of someone telling a story to a child.

"And you don't have to watch one single one of them die. You simply sit in comfort thousands of miles from the battlefield and ... "

Here he leaned forward and pressed Sally's nose lightly.

" ... press a button."

Sally rubbed her nose with her sleeve. Berthold looked puzzled.

"Where's the fun in that?"

Vulcan tapped the side of his head knowingly.

"Oh, we cater for all tastes here. You'd be surprised."

"It'll never sell! It's unnatural! It's unchivalrous!"

Sally looked at the Baron. She'd never heard him sound shocked before. Vulcan laughed.

"It'll sell all right, but it's a bit before its time. It won't go into production, that one, for another couple of hundred years. Come and have some fodder."

## 2

Vulcan's dining room fascinated Sally. To begin with, in contrast to Vulcan, it was clean. But what she liked most about it was that it made her feel a little sick. It reminded her of the time when she'd eaten too much chocolate. Violet would have said that it was vulgar. She couldn't recall having enjoyed disliking something in quite this way before. It was a nice feeling, but clearly one to be indulged in with care.

The room was full of gold furniture with what looked like diamond chandeliers hanging from the ceiling all reflected in tall mirrored walls. In one corner a little gold fountain bubbled into a big fat marble lily pond. In the middle of the room, on a gaudy mosaic floor, stood a marble-topped table inlaid with yet more gold. This was set for tea with tiny porcelain cups and saucers.

The one thing in the room which Sally did like and liked liking was a large rather fine brown cow standing next to the pond. This was intriguing. But what was even more intriguing was that nobody mentioned it, though Sally was sure that everybody knew it was there. She'd seen Berthold see it and do a double take and yet he hadn't said anything. Sally came very close to saying something, but decided not to in case the answer was so ordinary, like "It's there to provide milk for the tea," that it would spoil it. Having made up her mind not to ask she began to dread being told anyway.

The Baron guided a tiny teacup through his moustache and sipped the meager contents.

"Mmm . . . delicious."

Vulcan tipped his head back and threw his tea down his throat like a Russian drinking vodka. The miniature cup looked absurd in his big coal-blackened hands. He replaced it carefully in its saucer. Sally was sure he'd already broken several. She wished that whoever was bringing the food would get a move on.

"Yes, not a bad little tea as teas of the Gods go."

Vulcan wiped his mouth with a corner of his apron making his face dirtier than before. Sally was full of admiration. Here was one reason for wanting to be a God which had never occurred to her. The right to be as dirty as you liked. Vulcan poured everyone more tea.

"You can stay here for as long as you want. It's nice to have a bit of fresh company. One loses one's initial enthusiasm for conversation with Cyclopes after a few millennia."

The Baron picked up his replenished cup.

"Thank you. It would be a great pleasure."

Sally cleared her throat noisily.

"I'm sorry, but we have to go soon."

She glared sternly at the Baron.

"We're in a hurry."

Just then a door opened and a huge elderly butler entered pushing a gold trolley covered with plates of dainty miniature cakes. Vulcan's face lit up.

"Ah, my midget manservant with the petit fours."

Sally stared in horror and disbelief at the inadequate supply of silly little cakes. Perhaps the Gods didn't get enough to eat? Dirty but hungry.

The not-so-midget manservant had begun to pass the petit fours around when the Baron, quickly followed by Berthold, jumped to his feet.

"Albrecht!"

"Albrecht!"

They threw their arms around him. Sally took her eyes off the petit fours and looked at the servant. He was big and black and looked exactly like Bill the actor, or at least exactly like Bill playing Albrecht. The only difference being that this man was old and gray and it didn't look like make-up.

Albrecht, for it was indeed he, fell back under the combined assault of the Baron and Berthold.

"Baron! Berthold! What are you doing here?"

The Baron clasped Albrecht's hand.

"Looking for you."

A shifty expression appeared on Albrecht's face, reminding Sally of Bill on the day he lost everyone's wages at dice.

"I haven't got the treasure any more. I've spent it. Er . . . I mean, I gave it all to charity."

The Baron patted him on the back.

"I don't want the treasure."

He waved at Sally.

"This is Sally. Sally, Albrecht."

Sally swallowed her petit fours, having decided that their name indicated the quantity you were supposed to eat at one time.

"Hello."

She shook Albrecht's white gloved hand. He might be old, but he was still big and looked strong. He would certainly be able to help. The Baron, not familiar with Sally's etiquette, picked up five petit fours.

"We want you to come and help us fight the Turk again."

Albrecht fiddled with his white pinafore.

"Oh . . . I couldn't do that. Not now. Not since I found myself."

He began pouring tea. Sally looked at the Baron who looked at Berthold who looked at Albrecht's white lace cap. Albrecht blushed.

"I'm sorry. No. I know now that I never wanted to be big and strong. All I really wanted was to be gentle and sensitive and not have to lug heavy things about. They call me their midget down here. I love it. It's bliss."

He watered the diminutive teapot. Berthold leaned over to the Baron.

"He's gone funny."

The Baron had no time to consider this proposition before a strange wind began to blow through the dining room. It sounded like music. At the same time from somewhere unseen came music which sounded not unlike wind.

The Baron, Sally and Berthold looked to Vulcan who smiled wistfully and turned towards the lily pond in which the water level was rising and where waves were beginning to wash gently back and forth.

As the music swelled something broke the surface of the water. It took Sally a few moments before she recognized a gigantic scallop shell, the two halves of which were shut tight. Water cascaded off it as it gradually emerged, to come to rest with its closed mouth uppermost. The front half of the shell now fell slowly away to reveal, standing sedately in its center, a beautiful woman, naked, and swathed in long blond hair.

Sally instantly thought that this must be Lady Godiva, also that she looked remarkably like Rose the actress whose good looks she most admired and envied.

Two pretty handmaidens now materialized out of the blue carrying silken robes. They flew across the dining room and swooped around the beautiful woman, draping her with the shimmering material. The beautiful woman then sat in the middle of the shell with a handmaiden on either side of her. She smiled at the assembled company.

"Hello."

Sally was impressed that someone as sensationally beautiful as this who lived in a shell and who had flying servants could say anything as simple and straightforward as "hello." Vulcan was evidently even more impressed. He shuffled towards her looking as though he were about to fall onto his knees.

"Darling, dearest, this is Baron Munchausen and his friends Sally and Berthold."

He turned to the Baron.

"This is my wife, Venus. The Goddess."

Venus smiled seraphically. The Baron shot to his feet and bowed so low that Sally feared he might not come up again.

"Madam, I am overwhelmed."

Vulcan fumbled in the pocket of his apron.

"My love, my life, the alpha and omega of my existence, here, here ... "

He produced a large lump of what looked like coal, and taking a deep breath began to crush it with both hands. There was a crackling noise and a flash of light from the coal after which Vulcan opened his hands to reveal a big gleaming crystal on his grimy sweating palm.

"There's a diamond for you, my precious."

He offered it to Venus, who took it and pecked him on the cheek.

"How sweet. Another diamond."

She passed it to a handmaiden who added it to a pile of similar diamonds on the floor. The Baron was agog.

"Madam, I am, alas, unable to offer you so splendid a gift."

There was a tremor in his voice.

"But allow me to say that you excel in beauty even the magnificent Catherine the Great of Russia ... "

Berthold sighed and whispered to Sally.

"Here we go."

" ... whose hand in marriage I once had the honor to decline."

Venus lowered her eyes flirtatiously.

"Baron, you flatter me."

The Baron stood to attention.

"Not one jot madam, not one tittle."

Venus stepped out of her shell and approached him.

"What a handsome moustache."

She took him by the hand and led him away from the others.

"Shall we dance?"

From the next room came the sound of an orchestra playing a waltz.

Sally watched the Baron and Venus move across the dining room as if on wheels. They were looking fixedly into each other's

*"How sweet. Another diamond."*

Soon though, Berthold's lack of stamina caught up with him and he began to flag.

"Sally!"

The sweat was pouring off him. He contrived to sound jolly.

"You can dance, can't you?"

"No."

He gave her a venomous look.

"Thanks."

He kept going, but at a quarter the tempo.

Sally had begun to think that they shouldn't be wasting time protecting the Baron. If Vulcan was cross with him she was twice as cross. They were supposed to be on a rescue mission, not waltzing around the ceiling. She would insist that he come down and then they could go. Leaving Berthold in some distress, she marched into the ballroom and followed a path between the pools and fountains until she was beneath the Baron and Venus, who were now dancing inches from the clouds and cherubs painted on the ceiling. Sally squinted up at them, fountain spray falling in her face.

"Hey! Stop! Come down! We've got to go!"

The Baron was gazing rapturously into Venus' eyes. Sally noted that he looked even younger than before.

"Hey! Please! It's time to go!"

At last, as he made a turn, the Baron glanced down before spinning away.

"Don't fret! The town is in no immediate danger!"

### 3

Meanwhile, back at the siege, the townsfolk were working feverishly to reinforce the barricades and strengthen the gates which the Turks were endeavoring to smash down with a formidable battering ram. Things looked blacker than ever.

4

Sally, dissatisfied with the Baron's assurances, watched the dancers sweep back and forth under the painted sky. She was soaking wet now and furious. Why didn't they kiss each other? They looked as though they might. If only they'd kiss each other she'd have something to go and tell Vulcan. The Baron and Venus, still waltzing, moved inexorably closer and kissed. Now the painted sky came alive. The clouds moved. It had become a real sky. The winged cherubs too came to life, diving and fluttering around the embracing couple. Sally turned and ran to the dining room.

Here Berthold was attempting to keep his Vulcan-distracting dance going from a prostrate position on the floor. He looked extremely uncomfortable and rather ill. Vulcan was plucking fretfully at his beard. His fascination with Berthold's choreography seemed to be waning. Sally spoke loudly and clearly.

"The Baron's kissing your wife!"

On hearing this Berthold went rigid and lay still while Vulcan turned white then black and then white again and smoke began to trickle from the top of his head. He stormed towards the ballroom followed by Sally, who was now wondering whether or not she'd done the right thing.

In the ballroom the Baron and Venus were now at an even higher altitude, dancing among the white clouds. Two winged cherubs circled them with a long satin banner. The Baron, looking extremely young, produced a red paper rose and proffered it to Venus. It was a most exquisitely beautiful and moving moment.

"Harlot!"

Vulcan's harsh cracked voice boomed up from the ballroom floor. The white clouds and blue sky turned instantly to storm gray. The music stopped. The cherubs took fright and fled, dropping the satin banner with which they had entwined the waltzing couple so that one end of it fell within Vulcan's reach. He snatched it and wrenched it hard, dragging the Baron and Venus unceremoniously out of the sky.

"That's enough of that!"

The star-struck couple crashed onto the ballroom floor where Vulcan tried to disentangle them from the banner.

"You strumpet!"

Flames shot out from the bottoms of his trousers. Venus tried to calm him.

"Darling."

"Don't you 'darling' me, you hussy!"

He pulled her free and turned to the Baron.

"And as for you ...!"

He lifted the Baron above his head with one hand. Berthold, who'd watched all this in horror from the ballroom door, turned to Albrecht.

"Do something! Save him!"

"Er ... "

Albrecht dithered. He was experiencing the problem of divided loyalties. On the one hand he was pleased to see the Baron, his old master. On the other hand the Baron really ought not to turn up like this and immediately start making trouble. On the one hand he now worked for Vulcan and liked his new master. On the other hand perhaps Vulcan was a little bit out of order and going just a tiny bit over the top in the rough way he was treating the Baron. On the one hand that already added up to four hands so what was a person to do?

Vulcan, still carrying the Baron, stormed into the dining room with Venus in hot pursuit.

"Darling! Please! Don't be jealous!"

"I'm not jealous!"

He was still emitting flames and smoke. Venus struck at him with a long silken sleeve.

"You never let me have any friends!"

Berthold hid behind Albrecht and nudged him sharply. Albrecht dithered again.

"Er . . . "

Vulcan strode towards his workshop knocking over the gold trolley and scattering petit-four wrappers and lace doilies left and right.

"I won't have you wiggling at philanderers! You floozy!"

It is perhaps a measure of the Baron's greatness that, even at a moment of personal discomfort such as this, his prime concern was to protect the honor of the lady. This was certainly his own view.

"Sir, I assure you . . . "

But Venus was in full spate.

"I'm a Goddess, I can do what I like!"

"And I'm a God, so shut up!"

Vulcan exited into the workshop. The others raced after him.

In a corner of the workshop, surrounded by giant steam hammers, was a fast-moving whirlpool.

Vulcan carried the Baron to the edge of this with the clear intention of throwing him in. The Baron, clutching the red paper rose which he'd been prevented from giving Venus, attempted to twirl his moustache.

"I must insist that the lady is blameless."

Vulcan glared into the Baron's upside-down face.

"Ungrateful mortal!"

Berthold shoved Albrecht forward.

"Er . . . "

He began to dither again. Berthold poked him in the ribs.

"Er, sir. Vulcan. Excuse me . . . "

Berthold gave him another jab.

"Er, why don't we all just sit down quietly and . . . "

Vulcan heaved the Baron into the maelstrom. As the Baron sailed through the air the satin banner, in which he was still entangled, billowed out behind him. Albrecht caught the end of it.

"Now let's not be too hasty . . . Ahhh!"

The Baron's momentum carried Albrecht after him into the whirlpool where they both vanished.

Sally was appalled. What had she done? She turned to Vulcan.

"What have you done?"

He ignored her. Venus now screamed at him with a volume and tone not necessarily predictable from those lovely lips.

"You small-minded petit bourgeois . . . "

"Shut up, you trollop!"

Sally looked at Berthold in despair. He tapped Vulcan gingerly on the shoulder.

"What have you done with the Baron?"

He didn't sound as if he genuinely wanted an answer, but Vulcan grabbed him by the scruff of the neck anyway, and lifting Sally up with the other hand, threw them both into the whirlpool.

"You want the Baron! You can have the Baron!"

Vulcan and Venus were now left alone together, apart from three hundred or so Cyclopes who'd retired to the other end of the workshop and who didn't really count anyway, not being Gods. Venus drew close to Vulcan.

"Did you enjoy that? Did I excite you?"

Vulcan's eyelids began to flutter.

"Yes . . . very much."

His voice sounded warm and gooey. He took Venus in his arms and kissed her passionately whereupon all the giant furnaces roared into flame and the great steam hammers began to beat in symbolic approval.

*"An island."*

# PART X

# THE SOUTH SEAS

*The Baron becomes old again. Sally spies an island. Swallowed by a fish.*

## 1

hen Sally was thrown into the vortex she took a deep breath, closed her eyes and hoped for the best. This was either the end or they were moving on. She didn't really think it could be the end because it didn't seem like a proper end and there were still things to do. If it was the end then it was certainly a very untidy and unsatisfactory one. But then maybe it wasn't her story, or even the Baron's story, and perhaps it was a good ending for whoever's story it was. Vulcan for instance, or Horatio Jackson, or the King of the Moon, or somebody somewhere she'd never met or even heard of. She might be just a small part of some other bigger story. She was trying to make up her mind whether this notion was worrying or comforting when the thunderous rush of foam all around her ceased and things became quiet and still.

Sally was running out of breath. Her heart was beating fast as she tried hard not to inhale liquid. She opened her eyes. There, not far away, were the blurred outlines of the Baron, Berthold and Albrecht, floating with their legs dangling out into a void and all struggling to stay in the safety of the flood. Sally found herself doing the same thing. The void felt cold and looked blue and threatening. Just when she thought she was going to burst she saw a fish swim past upside down. Quickly righting herself she stuck her head into the void and took a huge breath of air. She was in the sea and what she had taken to be a void was the air, wind and sky above. The others were still fighting, legs in the air, to stay in the water. She paddled over and pushed them the right way up.

Berthold, at first delighted to be able to breathe, soon fell to grumbling.

"Help! I can't swim!"

The Baron and Albrecht looked miserable and just floated lethargically. Sally squeezed the salt water from her eyes.

"What's happening?"

She looked more carefully at the Baron.

"You've gone old again."

He seemed to have reverted to the age he'd been when she'd first seen him.

"Well, what do you expect!"

He was still holding the rose, now waterlogged, intended for Venus.

"I've just been expelled from paradise, and it's all your fault!"

Sally looked around. All she could see as far as the horizon in every direction was cold, wet sea.

"Where are we?"

The Baron didn't reply. He stared sullenly at the rose. Sally was shivering. She splashed him.

"Answer me!"

He lay back in the water.

"The most probable explanation, if you're not an incurable skeptic, is that we've fallen through the center of the world and come out on the opposite side. Somewhere in the South Seas."

"But that's miles away!"

Sally was dismayed. The Baron shut his eyes.

"It's as good a place to die as any."

"I was happy in my volcano!"

Albrecht was wretched.

"Anyone keen to win a medal for life-saving?"

Berthold kept disappearing beneath the surface in an alarming sort of way. Albrecht waited for him to bob up again.

"Don't struggle. Float naturally."

"I don't float naturally! I sink naturally!"

He sank again.

At that moment Sally spotted something long and low on the horizon.

"Look!"

The others turned to where Sally was pointing.

"An island!"

She wondered why she hadn't seen it before. Albrecht perked up.

"Is there a volcano on it?"

"Oh shut up about your poxy volcano!"

Berthold slid back beneath the waves.

As Sally tried to push herself higher in the water to get a better view she saw, about two thirds of the way along the island, something shoot up into the air.

"I think it has got a volcano!"

Then, to her horror, she became aware that it, whatever it was she was watching, was changing shape.

"It's moving!"

One end of the vast dark mass rose out of the water and then submerged as the other end began to rise, continuing upwards until what looked like an eye broke the surface and stared at them over the waves.

"I spy with my little eye something beginning with 'M'."

Berthold was dog-paddling in the opposite direction, but remaining in the same spot. Albrecht's eyes grew almost as large as the unblinking eye which was watching them across the water.

"It's a demon of the deep!"

"Demon starts with 'D,' you klutz! 'M'! 'M' for monster!"

Berthold paddled faster and looked as though with proper training he could become a very good swimmer indeed.

The creature changed shape again. The eye seemed to melt

away. What remained above water became arched and rounded before a great triangular fin appeared and traveled across it from right to left. Within moments the thing had vanished leaving scarcely a ripple. Sally spoke everyone's thoughts.

"Will it eat us?"

The Baron replied with his own.

"With any luck."

Nobody had a chance to say or think anything else before vast, pink, fleshy walls framed with razor-sharp teeth erupted from the surrounding water and engulfed them completely.

The giant fish closed its jaws on its prey, swung back into the sea and dived to the depths.

*"We've got to get him warm and dry."*

# PART XI

# THE FISH

*Fish food. A distant light, a funny noise and a horrid smell.*
*Reunion. Sally sees death and lectures the Baron. The horse*
*from the bowels of the fish. The big sneeze.*

## 1

hen Sally regained her senses she was lying in a shallow pool of water clinging to a length of rotten wood. At first she thought she was dreaming. She looked about her. There seemed to be no sure way of proving that she wasn't. The light was dim and it took her some moments to adjust. The wood that she was holding was covered with barnacles and extended high above her. It was connected to other pieces of wood in a curved frame which looked like the ribs of a large, ancient shipwreck. Sally stood up coughing sea water from the back of her throat. That seemed fairly un-dreamlike. Also there was a most dreadful smell, though perhaps that qualified for the category of nightmare. She kept losing her balance as the ground constantly shifted and tilted. Could she really be inside a fish, like Jonah? Looking up through the struts of the shipwreck she saw, high above, what she thought might be the upper part of the fish's stomach, undulating and streaming with moisture.

The sound of groaning sent her searching between the rotting timbers. Nearby, under a pile of seaweed, she found Berthold, half drowned, but still alive. Not far from him was Albrecht, who was upset because his pinafore and lace cap had shrunk. She looked around for the Baron. Surely the fish hadn't neglected to swallow Baron Munchausen? How could they be in one of his adventures without him? Berthold waved at her and pointed to the other end of the shipwreck. There was the Baron hanging inert from a broken spar. Sally waded over to him, but needed the others to lift him down. They joined her as quickly as they could and lowered him onto the ground. Albrecht turned him on his side.

"I think he's dead."

Sally wasn't having this.

"He can't be dead!"

The Baron moaned obligingly and started to cough. Albrecht, though pleased to have been wrong, didn't want it to be thought that his diagnosis had been totally without foundation.

"He's not very perky, is he?"

Berthold was so delighted at not having drowned that he felt compelled to make a joke.

"Is there a doctor in the fish?"

Berthold was the only one to laugh and the Baron became quite agitated.

"No doctors, no doctors!"

Sally remembered him having been upset in the theater when Jackson had mentioned doctors. She wondered whether he'd ever had an earache or had to take unpleasant medicine. He sniffed at the rose, which somehow or other he'd managed to keep hold of, and passed out. Sally wrung the water from the sleeves of her dress.

"We've got to get him warm and dry."

Hearing herself speak with such authority she half expected Albrecht and Berthold to take umbrage. They didn't. She thought this must be how cats felt picking up kittens by the scruffs of their necks. She was surprised at how easy it was.

Albrecht raised a finger.

"What's that noise?"

They listened. From somewhere far away or from inside something, for it seemed muffled, they could hear what sounded like a human voice. The noise it was making was horrible, like a badly sung dirge. It was all on two notes.

Trying to locate where it was coming from, Sally was the first to see a faint yellow light, flickering in the distance, apparently close to the stomach roof.

Berthold and Albrecht lifted the Baron and following Sally set off towards the source of the curious caterwauling.

## 2

The journey across the floor of the fish's stomach was a fairly disgusting one. Apart from the vile, persistent and all-pervading smell, the stomach lining was spongy and unpleasant to walk on and every now and then emitted jets of liquid.

"Digestive juices."

Berthold seemed to know a lot about fish. He said that he was a fish-man who in general preferred fish to red meat though in the case of this particular fish he might make an exception.

As they approached the light, and the noise was getting louder, they discovered that both were coming from the top of a tangled stack of wrecked ships. Trekking around the base of these wrecks Sally, with Berthold and Albrecht who were finding the Baron increasingly difficult to carry, came across a series of gangplanks and stairways leading up inside. They rested for a few moments before beginning the ascent towards the singing, which they could now identify as almost certainly human.

## 3

At the end of an exhausting climb, during which they saw no signs of life, Sally, Berthold and Albrecht, still carrying the Baron, arrived, breathless, at a door marked "Captain's Cabin."

A light shone from under it and the excruciating sound of someone slaughtering a bad sea shanty was rattling its handle.

"Oh once I had a sweetheart,

A sweetheart once I had,

She was the fairest beauty true,

Her eyes were like the ocean blue,

But her name was Davy Jones, O,

Her name was Davy Jones."

Sally waited for the singer to draw breath and knocked on the door.

"Oh once I had a sweetheart,

A sweetheart once I had,

She was the fairest beauty true,

Her eyes were like the ocean blue,

But her name was Davy Jones, O

Her name was Davy Jones."

The Baron groaned. Sally knocked harder.

"Oh once I had a sweetheart,

A sweetheart once I had . . . "

The singer went on. Obviously there wasn't a lot to be gained in this part of the world by observing the niceties of polite behavior. Sally turned the handle and opened the door.

The sight which met their eyes was not an ordinary one. Unless you happen to be a sailor who's been swallowed by a fish.

The cabin was large by sailing ship standards, with a low-beamed ceiling covered with the ubiquitous barnacle. In the middle, sitting around a circular table, a group of ancient mariners were playing cards. Light from candles on the table revealed their grizzled features and threw jagged shadows onto the paneled walls. In the corner furthest from the door could be seen the singer, who had a dead candle stump in each ear. Right in front of the door, facing them as they looked in was a seated figure which chilled the blood. It was completely encased in cobwebs, and although the cobwebs moved in and out where one might suppose the mouth to be, indicating that it was still breathing, spiders of all sorts and sizes had free run of it and could be seen moving back and forth undisturbed. Sally took a deep breath and stepped in, followed by the others.

"Excuse me. Hello ... "

"Oh once I had a sweetheart,
A sweetheart once I had ... "

Sally spoke louder.

"Excuse me ... "

"She was the fairest true beauty,
Her lips were red as red could be ... "

Sally shouted.

"We've just been swallowed and we need some help!"

"No doctors, no doctors!"

The Baron was beginning to revive.

"But her name was Davy Jones, O,
Her name was Davy Jones."

Sally wondered how any of them could stand this dreadful racket.

One of the card players, wearing much-repaired spectacles with cracked lenses and seeming to be nine parts blind, was holding his cards back to front. This man's hand was being played for him by his neighbor, who was clearly taking advantage of the opportunity to cheat.

The moment the Baron muttered about doctors the old man with the glasses cocked an ear and turned to his companion.

"Do I hear the Baron?"

His voice was so ruined that Sally couldn't understand a word, and neither, apparently, could the companion who, it now transpired, was deaf.

"Eh?"

The man with the glasses spoke again, this time more forcefully.

"I think it's the Baron."

The companion, who'd been staring in the direction of the new arrivals, stood up, or rather, stood down, since when he got off his chair he was seen to be very short.

"I think it's the Baron!"

This statement from the short man seemed to incense the man with the glasses who lifted a horn-like object from the table and hit him with it.

"That's what I just said! Use your trumpet!"

The small deaf man escaping from the blows of the angry blind one rushed forward to Sally and the others.

"Baron!"

He grasped the Baron's hand.

"Berthold! Albrecht!"

The Baron, much to the relief of Berthold and Albrecht, insisted on being put on his feet.

"Gustavus! Is it really you?"

They embraced.

"And Adolphus!"

He waved over at the blind man who was excitedly saying things which nobody could understand or even hear above the noise of the singer.

"... Jones, O, Her name was Davy Jones."

Albrecht began to weep.

"I don't believe it!"

Berthold threw his arms around Gustavus, for it was indeed he, crushing the little man's big ears against his solar plexus.

"You've got taller!"

He then guided Adolphus, for it was indeed he too, over from where he'd been lurching around embracing all the wrong people.

Sally just about recognized Gustavus and Adolphus from the Sultan's Tale when they'd been much younger. They reminded her of Jeremy and Rupert who played Gustavus and Adolphus for her father. It was a joyful reunion.

Sally was impressed that the Baron, in spite of everything, had succeeded in gathering all his servants, but she continued to fret about the fact that they were all now old and feeble, something which the Baron seemed determined to ignore.

Adolphus, having embraced everybody in the room at least three times, with the exception of the singer, collapsed onto a stool.

"So, you're dead at last, eh?"

Gustavus had his trumpet to his ear.

"We were beginning to think you might be immortal."

Sally was shocked. Perhaps it wasn't either real or a dream. Perhaps they were indeed dead.

"We're not dead!"

Berthold winced as the singer increased his volume.

"Sally, this is Adolphus, who used to be able to hit a bull's-eye halfway around the world, and Gustavus, who could blow down a forest with one breath."

Adolphus laughed like a narrow, badly maintained drain.

"Those were the days, eh? When we were young and alive."

"You're not dead!"

It occurred to Sally that spending too long in a fish addled one's brains.

"But her name was Davy Jones, O,

Her name was Davy Jones."

This song certainly didn't help. She looked at the Baron. He was moping over the battered rose. She touched Adolphus' elbow.

"How can we get out of here?"

Adolphus was puzzled.

"Out?"

Gustavus switched his trumpet to the other ear.

"You can't get out! You're dead."

Albrecht seemed to hear this for the first time.

"How do you mean?"

Adolphus sighed, as if he'd been through it all countless times before.

"It's no good fighting it."

"Oh once I had a sweetheart . . . "

Sally was getting desperate. She shouted.

"We're not dead!"

Gustavus removed the trumpet from his ear, clearly offended that Sally should think him deaf.

"We all die y'know. You have to accept it. We're all dead here. This is hell."

"Heaven!"

Adolphus thumped the table. Here was evidently a domestic disagreement with a history. Gustavus snapped back.

"Purgatory!"

Sensing that this might be a debate with perhaps limited appeal, at present, for the newcomers, Adolphus struck a conciliatory note.

"One of those places, anyway."

"Don't be stupid."

Sally felt it important not to give ground on this subject, even at the risk of being thought rude.

At this moment the singer suddenly stopped, clutched at his chest and fell onto the floor. The silence that followed was exquisite. Berthold rushed over to the supine soloist and listened to his chest. Sally hoped fervently that he might be dead. Berthold got up.

"He's dead."

Sally felt dreadful. Berthold covered the ex-singer with a piece of sacking.

"*He's* dead! Just now!"

Adolphus groped around the table for his cards.

"No. He's gone back to life again. He'll be a miracle now, up there in the land of the living. 'Til they get sick of the boring old git."

He patted the chairs on either side of him.

"Sit down, relax, have a game. You're dead for a very long time."

To Sally's annoyance the Baron sat down without hesitation, followed by Berthold and Albrecht. The cards were collected and passed to the dealer. Sally watched unhappily.

"What are you doing?"

The Baron ignored her. The dealer shuffled the cards, cut them and began to deal. Sally looked at the Baron more closely. His head hung forward, the skin on his face and neck was dry and heavily wrinkled, the muscles around his mouth and jaw were slack and his eyelids drooped. She recalled the time in the theater when she'd seen the ghastly creature kneeling on his chest.

"You're giving up again, aren't you?"

The Baron paid no attention. Sally recognized the extent and power of her responsibility.

"You can't give up! I won't let you!"

"Go away! Clear off!"

The Baron turned his back to her and began arranging his cards. She saw that he held the queen, jack and ace of spades. She also saw the damaged rose in his pocket.

"What about Rose and my father and all the others?"

She moved around to face him.

"You promised to save them!"

"They're all perfectly safe!"

4

Meanwhile back at the siege, the great gates of the city were starting to splinter and yield under repeated batterings by the Turks. It was beginning to look like the end.

## 5

Sally eyed the Baron skeptically. He swung away from her again.

"They can look after themselves."

She stepped around the chair to face him as before. He seemed almost mischievous.

"Besides. There are more important things."

She felt that he was trying to provoke her.

"Such as?"

He took the rose from his pocket and passed it under his nose. "Well..."

He tapped his fingers on the table. A card sliced, spinning, through the air and landed in front of him. It was the joker. For the first time Sally looked at the dealer. He was sitting in an inexplicable shadow. To begin with she thought he was smiling at her. Then she caught sight of his hands. They were thin and white and consisted entirely of bone. She looked back to the face. Now she could make out the row of long teeth, unobscured by lips, and the sunken eye socket empty of eyes.

Sally screamed and knocked the Baron's cards out of his hand. Everyone at the table jumped back, startled. The candle flames lay flat and nearly expired before returning upright, momentarily brighter than before. The dealer had gone. Sally spun around quickly and glanced under the table. No sign. The Baron caught her by the arms, shook her and pulled her close to his face.

"You horrible little brat!"

His eyes, narrow at first, opened wide as he began to shout.

"Can't you let me die in peace once in a while?"

Sally had never seen him so angry before, or so unlike himself.

His voice thundered around the cabin rattling the remaining leaded window panes. Scarcely had it died away when an echo or reply was heard from somewhere below decks. A strange fluctuating noise which began on a high note and then fell away. This was heard twice and was then followed by what sounded like running feet. Several, hard, heavy, clumsy feet, running quickly.

The congregation in the cabin looked at each other with growing fear. Whatever it was was traveling back and forth along the gangways within the ship and climbing stairs. It seemed to be heading for them.

The Baron let go of Sally and steered her towards Berthold and Albrecht, who took her, with the others, as far away as possible from the door. He pulled the table from the middle of the room, positioning it to one side and slightly behind him where the light from its candles would give him the advantage over whatever entered. He threw the stools and chairs in front of the others to provide them with some protection. Then he drew his sword, placed his feet firmly apart, and swaying slightly, waited. Nobody spoke.

The running feet continued their wild, pounding, inexorable progress towards the cabin until it seemed that they were right outside. Here they stopped abruptly for a second before a tremendous banging began. Violent blows shook the cabin. The Baron raised his sword, but lowered it again when he realized that the blows weren't being aimed at the door. Instead they were falling on the planking in the adjacent wall between two bunk beds. The Baron shifted his position while everyone else took cover behind a thin wooden ceiling support.

The terrifying blows to the wall continued until a section of wood disintegrated leaving a large hole through which stepped an elegant, white, Arab stallion. The Baron dropped his sword.

"Bucephalus!"

The horse whinnied and blew through its nose. The Baron threw his arms around its neck.

"Bucephalus! My Bucephalus!"

Bucephalus, for it was indeed he, nuzzled the Baron so vigorously that he nearly knocked him over.

"He must have heard me when I shouted at Sally!"

Everyone was immensely relieved, but it took them some moments before they relaxed sufficiently to come out from their inadequate shelter. Sally patted Bucephalus as the Baron inspected him thoroughly and patted Sally.

"This is a good omen, what?"

The Baron seemed quite recovered, quite his new self again. And Berthold too had cheered up, in a gloomy sort of way.

"Oh yeh?"

The Baron picked up his sword and put a hand on Berthold's shoulder.

"Prepare a rowing-boat and be ready to leave."

Berthold looked blank. A profound blankness which Sally had come to recognize as singularly Berthold's. The Baron laughed, sheathed his sword, opened the cabin window and, taking a snuff box from his waistcoat pocket, flipped up the lid and scattered the snuff out of the window into the innards of the giant fish.

"I have learned from experience that a modicum of snuff can be most efficacious."

Sally was thrilled. She felt sure she knew what was coming next. This was the line which her father, as the Baron, said in Act I just before he was expelled through the blowhole of the fish. It was amazing. What did it all mean? Sally recalled her father's line as Hamlet in Shakespeare's play. "There are more things in heaven and earth, Horatio, than are dreamt of in your philosophy." It was a rum business.

The Baron lifted what Sally recognized as Adolphus's musket from the corner and pressed it on Adolphus. He then covered his nose with his hand, indicated to the others that they should do the same, placed his hat over Bucephalus's nostrils and led everybody out through the door.

Before they'd reached the poop deck the giant fish had begun to tremble and shudder.

The mountain of wrecked ships rocked precariously. A spar bounding across the poop-deck balustrade would certainly have decapitated Sally and Gustavus had they been six inches taller. Having found a boat and climbed aboard, Albrecht put his large feet through the bottom if it. They scrambled out and found another, just in time.

## 6

The giant fish had been feeling rather queasy for years. Its health had been undermined by eating too many indigestible ocean-going vessels. In fact, it had come to the conclusion that there was no such thing as a digestible ocean-going sailing vessel and had decided that in the future it would stick to eating only tiny objects which did not have keels, rudders, masts or sails. It had been sticking rigorously to this diet when it had eaten Sally, the Baron, Berthold and Albrecht. Now it felt

decidedly pre-ulcerous. Its stomach was on fire and there was an unpleasant acidity in the back of its throat.

It dived to the bottom of the deepest sea it could find, took a mouthful, rolled over, swam like lightning to the surface, squeezed its lateral fins tightly against its sides and blew a mighty jet of water out through its blowhole.

Though this, at the time, was a rather uncomfortable exercise for the giant fish, it had already begun to feel a lot better in itself as huge sections of rotting ship with masts and keels splashed down into the water all around it.

It heaved a sigh of relief, flicked its tail and set off in search of microscopic plankton.

*"If you're still interested in my head, it's yours. I'm tired of it."*

# PART XII

# THE BATTLE

*More water. An amazing coincidence. A terrible rout. Sally is discouraged. The Baron plans the battle. Surrender? Horatio Jackson in disguise. The execution. Another close shave. The old gang deliver the goods. The victory parade.*

## 1

s a connoisseur of sub-aquatic journeys, Sally thought that the expulsion through the blowhole of the fish was marginally nastier than the trip from Vulcan volcano to the South Seas. She fervently hoped that this might be her last experience of such things. In the future she wanted to travel in comfort, even if it took a little longer.

On leaving the fish, everyone except Berthold fell out of the boat, so that when they splashed into the sea they had to swim around and search each other out. By a stroke of good fortune the rowing-boat had not sunk on landing or been damaged by the other flotsam and jetsam from the fish. Berthold helped the others on board. He took a deep breath.

"Fresh air! I'll never eat fish again. If they promise not to eat me."

"Where's the Baron?"

Sally peered around. Bucephalus was missing too. The sea was covered with fog and she could see only a few yards.

"Baron!"

Her voice seemed to fail in the mist.

"Baron!"

Silence.

"Baron!"

Berthold and Albrecht shouted. Nothing.

Sally could feel the tears making their way to her eyes. Was this really the way it was meant to happen? With her leading the others to victory without the Baron? She recognized this, guiltily, as an attractive thought. How difficult everything was. Berthold put his arm around her. Adolphus turned away.

Albrecht and Gustavus stared at the bottom of the boat. The tears reached her eyes. No, she wanted the Baron, victory or no victory.

"Baron!"

Concentric ripples appeared nearby, on the otherwise calm surface of the water. Sally saw them first and nudged the others.

Almost before they had time to suspend their disbelief, an arm appeared. It looked like the Baron's arm. It was, to everyone's astonishment. Sally thought that the others would have been used to such things. The Baron, gripping Bucephalus between his knees, pulled himself out of the sea by his own pigtail. He looked towards the boat.

"Well, come on! I can't keep this up forever!"

Having lifted himself and Bucephalus on board, the Baron took charge and persuaded the reluctant Albrecht to row them through the mist.

After a while they found themselves passing through shallow waters, between the masts of sunken ships. A slight breeze shifted the mist. Now Sally could see that they were in a familiar harbor close to the besieged town and within sight of the Turkish camp. She could hardly believe it.

"Look! We're back!"

The Baron pointed to the ragged flag still fluttering above the walls.

"And the flag's still flying! I told you there was nothing to worry about!"

Had Sally been able to reach him at that moment she was sure she would have hit him, but it was true that the assault on the town had ceased and the Turkish soldiers appeared to have returned to their tents.

A number of distant explosions and puffs of smoke heralded the arrival, within seconds, of Turkish cannonballs which began to splash into the water all around them. Now Berthold took the lead.

"Oh my Gawd! The Sultan's army! Quick! Back in the fish!"

A cannonball, closer than the others, sent a plume of water high into the air drenching Adolphus in the back of the boat. The Baron spoke calmly.

"They are inviting us to defeat them. We must oblige."

He drew his sword.

"On the count of three: Gustavus, blow them back to Asia Minor! Adolphus, find the Sultan and shoot him! Albrecht, pull for the shore! Berthold, make yourself useful! One! Two! Three!"

The Baron's crew of elderly followers looked at each other in impotent astonishment. Berthold lifted his hand.

"You couldn't make that four, could you?"

He was about to add something else when a cannonball tore through the middle of the boat and it began to sink. Sally felt the water creeping over her feet.

"We're going down!"

The Baron made a futile attempt to look as though he were still in control of the situation.

"Abandon ship!"

Berthold clung to the prow.

"I think the ship's abandoning us, mate!"

The two separate halves of what had been the rowing-boat drifted gently apart and sank, depositing the Baron and friends once again in the water. Berthold glowered at everyone.

"I still can't swim!"

The most exciting of adventures can have their trying moments for even the most intrepid adventurers. Such moments will almost certainly be induced by, among other things, becoming repeatedly wet. Regardless of how fascinating or glamorous the circumstances in which the protagonist may be plunged into water, he or she can be guaranteed sick to death with the whole business after the third immersion.

It was in just such a state of waterlogged dispiritedness that Sally, the Baron, Berthold, Gustavus, Albrecht, Adolphus and Bucephalus staggered out of the sea onto a stony beach in the shelter of an overhanging cliff some two miles from the Turkish camp.

The Baron's pockets and boots were full of water, making movement difficult, and the sodden feather in his hat drooped in front of his face.

"This is absolutely dreadful!"

Sally kicked at a pool of water.

"It's hopeless!"

She was very discouraged. Here they were, with all the Baron's servants, quite unable to do anything. The balloon and everything had been a complete waste of time. The Baron lay on the pebbles and held his legs in the air, draining the water from his boots.

"I've never before been in such a disastrous rout! I'm usually on the winning side!"

Albrecht floated in on the tide.

"If you weren't so competitive you wouldn't get so upset!"

He bumped into Berthold, who was lying on the water's edge. Berthold shoved him away.

"Albrecht's useless."

He looked up at Sally and nodded towards the Baron.

"I've been trying to tell him about my legs."

It seemed to Sally that Berthold was the only one prepared to acknowledge that there was a problem. Adolphus, clutching his musket with one hand and Gustavus with the other, toppled onto the shingle.

"Well, there's nothing wrong with us, is there, Gustavus!"

Gustavus shook a colony of crabs from his ear trumpet.

"Eh?"

Sally flopped down under the cliff, away from everyone.

"We might as well give up!"

This seemed to enliven the Baron. He pulled back his shoulders, twirled his moustache, and smiled at her.

"You mustn't say that! Not *you*."

Sally didn't smile back. He was so annoyingly contrary.

Gustavus and Berthold collected driftwood and built a fire in a cove out of sight of the Turkish camp in the hope that the smoke wouldn't be seen. Here they all huddled around, slowly drying out, with the exception of the Baron, who paced back and forth and then began to draw a map in the sand next to the fire with his sword.

"Now, if we begin attacking from two directions simultaneously, we compound surprise with confusion. Albrecht and Gustavus will provide the main themes, as it were, to the battle, while Adolphus and Berthold ... "

Sally prodded the fire.

"Baron."

"Don't interrupt!"

He flicked a pebble away with the point of his sword.

"What is it?"

She wiped her nose with her sleeve.

"This isn't going to work."

"What do you mean?"

Sally sighed. What did he mean what did she mean?

She indicated the others, who were manifestly in need of a holiday and a long rest.

"They're all old and tired. It's not like it used to be. Don't you see?"

For a moment Sally thought the Baron looked as though he might have seen. He contemplated his old servants in turn, frowned, kicked sand over his map and threw down his sword.

Sally made a place for him by the fire, but instead of sitting down he turned and set off at a brisk walk, across the cove, in the direction of the Turkish camp. Sally ran after him.

"Where are you going?"

The Baron kept moving.

"To give myself up."

"What?"

Sally was stunned. The Baron halted.

"I gave my word that I'd raise the siege and save the town!"

He was shouting. He looked towards the others around the fire.

"And I gathered you all together for that purpose!"

They stared back, dumbfounded.

"If you wish to see Baron Munchausen again you'll have to do something about it!"

He set off again with Sally at his heels.

"You can't give yourself up! They might kill you!"

The Baron stalked on. Sally stopped and watched him go.

"And then we'll have spent all that time in that smelly fish for nothing!"

The Baron marched so confidently into the Turkish camp, and the guards were so astounded at seeing him there that he went totally unchallenged. He saluted the soldiers, doffed his hat to the women and soon reached the Sultan's tent, easily identified by its size and magnificence, where he lifted the entrance flap and stepped inside.

Here, to his amazement, he found the Sultan in deep discussion with Horatio Jackson. He recognized Jackson in spite of the latter's long black cloak of disguise and dark smoked glasses. This was obviously a secret visit. They were both eating and drinking. Neither of them noticed the Baron. Jackson referred to a sheaf of papers and a calendar.

"So, on Friday the 28th, you surrender. That's three weeks from tomorrow. We can arrange the details later."

"No, no, no. *You* surrender."

The Sultan sucked a sugared almond. Jackson smiled uneasily and sipped wine from a glass.

"With respect, Sultan, we've been through all this. *You* surrender."

"But we're winning."

The Sultan ate a morsel of pigeon pie topped with layers of filo pastry. Jackson shifted uncomfortably on his cushion.

"We surrendered at the end of the last war."

"So?"

The Sultan placed a pickled prune in his mouth. Jackson tried to straighten his legs.

"So it's your turn."

The Sultan spat out the pickled prune.

"I still don't get it."

Jackson put his wine glass down and leaned on a bolster.

"Listen, if we surrender again, that's twice in succession. It all becomes terribly lopsided. Unbalanced. Whereas if you surrender, it's symmetrical."

The Sultan licked a crystallized fig.

"What about the virgins?"

Papers from Jackson's sheaf fell onto the carpet.

"Please. Forget about the virgins. We're out of virgins. Let us concentrate on reaching a rational, sensible, and civilized agreement which will guarantee a world fit for science, progress..."

"But not Baron Munchausen."

The Baron stepped forward.

"Baron!"

The Sultan jumped to his feet choking on a macaroon. Jackson ducked under his cloak of disguise, then re-emerged.

"You! The old lunatic!"

The Baron strolled toward them.

"I'm afraid so."

"Guards! Help! Murder!"

The Sultan seized a small gold tray and held it in front of him, scattering stuffed dates around the semi-tame tiger on the rug. Two dozen guards raced into the tent and quickly surrounded the unarmed Baron. The Sultan's eyes narrowed. He looked at his reflection in the polished tray and smoothed an eyebrow, as if that had always been his intention.

"How did this man get into my presence?"

The guards shook their heads and looked worried.

"Sultan ..."

The Baron sounded relaxed and cool.

"If you're still interested in my head, it's yours. I'm tired of it."

The Sultan slapped the gold tray as if it were a tambourine.

"Send for the executioner!"

A guard departed at the double. The Baron considered Jackson.

"So, Mr. Jackson, still the 'rational' man, eh? How many people have perished in your logical little war?"

Jackson's knees creaked and popped as he stood up with difficulty.

"There are certain rules, sir, to the proper conduct of living. We cannot fly to the moon. We cannot defy death. We must accept the facts and not the folly of fantasists like you who don't live in the real world and who consequently come to a sticky end."

The Sultan poured a glass of wine.

"A last drink, Baron? Excellent Tokay!"

## 2

The preparations for the Baron's execution were completed with speed and efficiency. The executioner's block was positioned on a raised platform where all might see, with the possible exception of the blind executioner, and seats and cushions were set in the porch of the Sultan's pavilion for the Sultan, Jackson and officials.

Both Baron and Sultan had too great a sense of delicacy to mention the treasure.

When the appointed hour had come the executioner's assistant measured and marked the Baron's neck, just as he had done in the Sultan's tale. Next to the scaffold a drummer beat out a slowly quickening pulse to add excitement and a sense of theater to the occasion for the benefit of those jaded observers who had witnessed too many executions in the past. The Sultan threw a spiced raisin into his mouth and called to the Baron.

"Do you have any famous last words?"

The Baron smiled.

"Not yet."

The Sultan was puzzled.

"'Not yet'?"

He turned to Jackson.

"Is that famous?"

Jackson looked away, hiding his contempt.

"The man's a buffoon."

The Sultan clapped his hands.

"Executioner!"

The executioner's assistant manhandled the executioner into position with scimitar raised, and invited the Baron to place his head on the block, which the Baron obligingly did. The volume and tempo of the drumming increased. The Sultan picked up a lump of Turkish delight and threw it at the executioner.

"Execute!"

The drumming reached a crescendo. The executioner leaned back, stretching on his toes, and started the scimitar on its death-dealing descent.

The razor-sharp blade had traveled about a foot, and the Baron was beginning to suspect that he might have made an error in judgment, when something hit it, making a sharp metallic noise and sending it spinning from the executioner's hands towards the Sultan where it sliced the top off his turban narrowly missing his scalp.

A mile away, on a precarious outcrop of rock, two curious-looking old men were cheering, hugging each other, and hopping up and down. One of them was Berthold and the other was Adolphus, who had just fired his musket and managed, with a supreme effort of concentration, to hit the executioner's blade.

Before the Sultan had recovered from the shock, Bucephalus, with the Baron's saber slung around the pommel of his saddle, leaped over eight rows of Turkish soldiers and galloped past the scaffold, enabling the Baron to vault onto his back. The Baron wheeled about, brandishing his saber and scattering the audience.

The Sultan screamed to his generals, who were sitting together and who jumped to their feet in unison, conveniently for the Baron, who rode past and cut off all their heads with one blow.

The Baron now fought his way on the willing and agile Bucephalus through a pack of guards to the entrance of the Sultan's pavilion where he cut guy ropes and poles, bringing the canopy down on top of the Sultan and Jackson, who'd retreated inside.

Here the Baron paused and raised his sword in salute to the tiny figures on the distant rock!

"I knew you could do it! All together now!"

He looked with relish at the approaching Turkish soldiers and plunged into the fray.

From a ridge of sand dunes half a mile inland, Sally, Albrecht and Gustavus had watched their plan unfold, at first with trepidation, but, after Adolphus's shot had found its mark, with jubilation and growing confidence.

When the Baron demolished the Sultan's pavilion, Gustavus judged it right to inhale a mighty lungful of air and blow it at the

Turkish camp. En route it whipped up clouds of blinding sand, and arrived to flatten tents, spook the horses and elephants, and generally throw the Turks into confusion and disarray.

Sally was overwhelmed, impressed and touched that the Baron's old and infirm servants had concentrated their minds and energies and were taking action to save their wayward master. Though it should be said that this had not been achieved without a certain amount of swearing and cursing and wishing the Baron to hell and kingdom come.

Gustavus's lung power was quite up to Sultan's Tale standards, but the first blast nearly finished him off and he was left wheezing, coughing and panting for breath. Sally tried to help by thumping him on the back.

During this moment, as the sand and dust settled, the Turks began to recover and once again assail the Baron. Twelve Turkish cavalry, their swords whirling, attacked and fell in quick succession, while a thirteenth, approaching the Baron from behind, raised his lance at close quarters, and had almost sent it thudding home when he flung his arms in the air and fell from the saddle.

The Baron turned, looked at him, then raised his hat to a little cloud of smoke on the rocky outcrop where Berthold was already helping Adolphus to reload his musket.

Meanwhile, in the sand dunes, Gustavus, with Sally's help, had managed to clear his bronchial tubes, and was starting to take a much-needed deep breath.

Air, sand, dust, and, from close by, small plants and cacti, roared into his open mouth. Further afield, in the Turkish camp, the remaining tents were sucked over, an elephant capsized, and whole platoons of soldiers, odalisques and eunuchs began to slip and slide in Gustavus's direction. Sally watched in trepidation as twenty or thirty spear-carrying soldiers were dragged, helplessly, out of the camp, across half a mile of scrub, and up the sand dune.

When these were only yards away, Gustavus reached the end of his inhalation. Now, bruised and angry, the soldiers got to their feet and began to advance menacingly at Sally, Gustavus and Albrecht. Gustavus tried to blow at them, but couldn't unblock his mouth and throat which were now packed with debris. The soldiers were almost upon them. Sally and Albrecht thumped and bashed Gustavus's back, but to no avail. There was only one thing for it. Sally pinched his nose, preventing him breathing altogether. One second, two seconds, at the third second Gustavus exhaled with hurricane force, blasting the soldiers high into the air.

At this moment, under the collapsed pavilion, the Sultan and Jackson had evaded the tiger and found their way to the edge of the canvas.

The Sultan stuck his head out, looked up into the gale, saw two dozen pike-carrying soldiers descending on him from the sky, and ducked back in again.

Jackson, however, marginally the more desperate of the two, made a break for it, and was fleeing through the devastated camp when he was spotted by the Baron, who tried to give chase, but was thwarted by a group of the Sultan's bodyguards.

While the Baron cut a swathe through the Janissaries, a Turkish sniper on top of one of the siege towers drew a bead on him.

Adolphus, seeing this from his rock promontory, aimed at the sniper and pulled his trigger. The musket failed to go off. Adolphus was frantic. There was nothing he could do. He

shouted at Berthold. Berthold looked stricken, then pulling himself together he ran off the rock on a cloud of dust with something approaching his old speed.

Berthold gritted his teeth and pumped his legs. They were absolutely killing him. He'd had folk-tale knee for the past fifteen years, and though some days were better than others, he didn't expect it ever to go away entirely. Not in his lifetime anyway.

Speeding towards the Turkish camp, Berthold could see the sniper on top of the tower. Would he get there in time? Or, perhaps what was more to the point, having got to the tower (he could still run, apparently) would he be able to get up it? He'd never had particularly strong arms, even in his heyday.

He was within a millisecond of the base of the tower when the sniper fired at the Baron. This, while not ideal, did at least solve the problem of the prospective climb, and it was with mixed feelings that he spun around on his suspect knees and rocketed after the musket ball.

He caught up with it when it was just over halfway to its target, took it between finger and thumb, then withdrew his hand rapidly. The damn thing was hot. He accelerated past it, whizzed to a halt between it and the Baron, snatched up a piece of discarded armor, held it in the path of the musket ball and deflected it harmlessly away. Harmlessly, that is, for the Baron, since the ball ricocheted off two spears, one after the other, and returned to the siege tower where it hit the sniper and knocked him to the ground.

The Baron, having pulverized the Janissaries, turned to discover Berthold lying exhausted in the sand. He flourished his saber.

"Dammit, man, make yourself useful! I can't do everything!"

The Baron and Bucephalus, almost as one, now performed an astonishing trick. They goaded the Turkish cavalry into chasing them around the camp at an ever-increasing speed and in ever-decreasing circles. At one point they were moving so quickly and so adroitly that there seemed to be several of them at once. The Turkish riders were mesmerized and stupefied. They were unable to catch up with the Baron and yet he seemed to be behind them.

The Baron led them into a tighter and faster circle until he and Bucephalus appeared to be spinning in the center like a top, while the Turkish cavalry collided with each other and spun dizzily out to crash uselessly into the sand.

Sally watched this display from the sand dunes with wonderment. It was like something choreographed for the theater.

She, Gustavus, and Albrecht gave the Baron and Bucephalus a standing ovation.

Sally then turned to Gustavus.

"Now, easy breaths this time."

If only she could get him to be more restrained. He might then be able to disrupt the Turks without half choking to death.

On the rocky outcrop, Adolphus, who was getting bored on his own, reloaded his musket, took aim and fired. The lead ball whistled into the Turkish camp, struck the trigger of a musket which had just been loaded by a Turkish soldier, fired it, sending a second lead ball into a large powder keg sitting, supposedly protected, beneath a pyramid of cannonballs. The powder keg exploded, throwing the cannonballs high into the air from where they fell back to cause more destruction and panic among the Turks, though two nearly landed on Adolphus.

One might have thought that all this would have been sufficient to convince the Turks that it was time to go home, but some of the braver or more reckless ones had begun to rally, and having located Gustavus, Sally and Albrecht on the sand dune started lobbing shells at them.

Albrecht seemed pleased when this happened. It gave him an excuse to join in. He was regretting his resolution not to do anything. In all the excitement and activity he'd even forgotten about his volcano. Now he stomped off across the sand to the harbor where he waded into the water, collected a dozen sunken ships by their anchor chains and began to swing them around his head.

While Albrecht was limbering up in the harbor, Gustavus had recruited a sand mouse which he blew gently out of Sally's hand so that it floated across the dunes and rolled to a halt in the Turkish elephant compound.

Contrary to Gustavus's belief, elephants are not frightened of mice, but as luck would have it these particular elephants were, having picked up the phobia from their trainer.

Seeing the tiny creature running around between their legs, the elephants, accustomed though they were to explosions, missiles, and frenzied cavalry charges, panicked and bolted through the camp trampling everything, except the mouse, underfoot.

Seeing Albrecht's ships swinging around and around in the sky above them, and Gustavus's elephants stampeding towards them, and Adolphus's cannonballs raining down on them, and the Baron riding pell-mell, unimpeded through their camp, the Turks decided to call it a day and began to retreat as quickly as possible.

The Sultan, still entangled under the canopy of his pavilion where he was being stalked by the angry tiger, had almost given up hope of rescue when one of the elephants, charging past, snagged the pavilion in its harness and dragged the whole thing, Sultan and all, behind it in a bundle. The tiger escaped and padded after the bundle licking its lips.

Any lingering doubts which the odd Turk might have had about the necessity for retreat were unquestionably resolved when Albrecht, having worked up considerable centrifugal force with his ships, let them go so that they sailed, disconcertingly, through the sky and smashed to earth in the wake of the departing army.

As the enemy disappeared in a cloud of dust, Sally and the others heard and saw crowds of citizens and soldiers cheering and waving to them from the top of the city walls. They waved back and ran into the wreckage of the Turkish camp to congratulate each other. Berthold climbed out from under the sand.

"We did it! We did it!"

"We've won!"

Gustavus came hurtling down a sand dune and promptly fell into a shell hole. Adolphus struggled in with his heavy musket.

"We beat them! We've done it!"

"Yahoo!"

Albrecht threw a cannonball into the air as if it were no more than an apple. Sally danced around the remains of a mortar cannon.

"Yippee! They've gone!"

"Good riddance! And don't come back!"

Adolphus waved his fist in the approximate direction of the retreating Turks. Sally turned to the Baron.

"We've won!"

She saw that he'd become young again.

"Of course!"

His sword arm twitched with the occasional involuntary fighting movement. Sally felt very proud. Proud of the Baron, the gang and herself. She'd believed in him when nobody else had and she knew it was this that had done the trick. Because she'd believed in his fantasies he'd been able to make them come true. He'd found his magical servants and together they'd saved the town. Berthold hopped up and down.

"We did it!"

He stopped suddenly and frowned.

"We *did* it? *We* did it?"

Gustavus climbed out of the shell hole.

"We've won?"

"How the hell did we manage that?"

Adolphus too was overcome with disbelief.

"With considerable reluctance!"

Albrecht dropped his cannonball and collapsed, exhausted, onto the sand. Adolphus, Gustavus and Berthold followed suit.

What none of them had seen, among the happy crowds on the battlements, was the sour face of Horatio Jackson.

### 3

The people threw open the gates and rushed out to welcome the conquering heroes. They were beaten to it by the Baron's faithful dog, Argus, who had waited impatiently for his master to return.

Everyone shook the Baron's hand until it nearly came off, embraced Sally so many times that the Baron had to lift her onto Bucephalus to prevent her from being crushed, hoisted Berthold, Gustavus, Adolphus and Albrecht onto their shoulders, and collected food abandoned by the Turks, before processing into the town.

Argus led the way, followed by the Baron and Sally on Bucephalus with Berthold, Gustavus, Adolphus and Albrecht directly behind them, and the remnants of the town band bringing up the rear. The streets were lined with jubilant crowds.

As they entered the square of the monument of the headless horse and headless rider, Sally saw that scaffolding had been erected around the statue and that the heads of both horse and rider were being winched back into place. She could hardly believe her eyes. They were unmistakably the heads, in bronze, of the Baron and Bucephalus. How could this be? And had it always been the case? Before she could turn to the Baron, she saw her father in the crowd. Daisy, Rose and Violet were with him. They were waving furiously and holding up a banner on which was written in a hurried scrawl: "Henry Salt and Daughter, Players." Sally waved back equally furiously, thinking that this must be the happiest as well as one of the most mysterious days of her life.

*"He took aim."*

## PART XIII

# THE DEATH OF THE BARON

*The sniper. Doctor Death. Sally fights back. A sad end.*

### 1

igh on the top of the cathedral tower overlooking the square, a hooded figure crouched behind a gargoyle carved in the semblance of a Winged Death. This was Horatio Jackson, and he was holding a loaded and primed musket. Below him he saw the procession circling around the monument. He calculated that all eyes were on the Baron and that the noise from the crowd and the band was such that no one would hear a single shot. He took aim. It would be difficult to hit the Baron from the front with the girl in the way. He would have to wait until they turned and shoot him in the back.

### 2

The procession was now about to make its third revolution of the square. The cheering crowd showed no signs of tiring. Sally was astonished by how many hats were still being thrown into the air. Where were they all coming from? Had people brought more than one hat for the occasion? Since they rarely seemed to fall back into the hands of whoever had thrown them, Sally deduced that people must have been catching or picking up and throwing other people's hats where they fell. Would everyone get their own hat back at the end? It was all very interesting. She heard a sudden gasp from the crowd. The band stopped playing. Somebody screamed. She turned and saw the Baron not sitting in the saddle behind her, but lying on the ground. More screams. People pushed, pressing towards him, others ran away, some pointing to the roofs of the surrounding buildings.

Sally slid down Bucephalus and forced her way through the crush to the Baron where she was joined by Berthold, Albrecht, Adolphus and Gustavus. Berthold examined the Baron, lifted his head and looked at the others.

"He's dying."

### 3

Jackson, having fired the fatal shot, hid behind the gargoyle.

He would leave the musket here and descend quickly to join the people.

While he was taking off his cloak the gargoyle broke its moorings, stretched its wings and dropped down to disappear into the crowd below.

Terrified by what he'd just witnessed, Jackson was left standing momentarily exposed. He recovered quickly and dodged back into the tower, but not before he'd been seen from the square. Soldiers began shooting at him.

### 4

Sally was in a state of shock. She stared at the Baron. His face was white. He looked as young as he had when dancing with Venus, and yet he was dying. Surely this couldn't be right? Daisy loosened the Baron's collar.

"Fetch a doctor! Hurry!"

Violet burst into tears.

"Don't leave me, Baron, please don't leave me!"

Rose eased her away.

"Give him air!"

Noticing that Sally was upset, Daisy took her by the arm and pushed her gently towards Salt.

"Mind Sally."

Salt took her aside. Someone in the crowd called out.

"Here's a doctor."

A path was made for a tall black-coated figure. Argus growled at him. The Baron stirred.

"No doctors, no doctors."

Sally saw the doctor lean over the Baron, throw back his cloak, kneel down and open his bag. Somebody passed in front of her, obscuring her view for a moment. When they'd moved aside she found herself looking at the winged figure of death. It was kneeling on the Baron's chest, had one skeletal hand on his

throat and with the other was beginning to extract something from his mouth. Sally screamed, tore herself away from her father and flew at the hideous creature. She'd rescued the Baron from it twice before and she would do so again.

"No! No! Get away! Leave him!"

She punched and kicked at it. It didn't respond. It didn't move. This was terrible. Hands were trying to drag her back. No one else seemed to see it. She screamed again.

"Go away! Stop! Leave him! Somebody help me!"

Salt and Daisy restrained her and pulled her away.

"Sally, what's the matter? What is it?"

She tried to get free of them.

"Look! Don't you see it? Stop it! Get it away!"

Salt held her firmly.

"Daisy, Violet, quick, help me! She's having a fit!"

Salt, assisted by Daisy and Violet, lifted the screaming, struggling Sally through the crowd as the hooded figure of death removed something glowing and fluttering from the Baron's mouth. Rose covered her face with her hands.

"He's dead."

Doctor Death moved away and was hurrying across the square when Argus caught up with him and snapped at his heels, causing him to trip. As he fell he dropped the glowing fluttering thing which flew, spiralling, high above the town where it appeared to dissolve into the sun.

"... he stopped, turned and waved before
disappearing over a ridge of sand."

# PART XIV

# LONG LIVE THE BARON

*The funeral. Applause. Jackson intervenes. The Baron leads the way. Salt rises to the occasion. All's well that ends well. The Baron rides again.*

## 1

On the day of the funeral the weather was suitably dreary, with a damp wind and gray sky threatening rain. Bucephalus followed directly behind the coffin with the Baron's boots fixed symbolically backwards in the stirrups. Behind Bucephalus came Sally with Argus and the others, all inconsolable. The same band which only days before had played a victory anthem now played a funeral march.

Sally, Berthold, Adolphus, Gustavus and Albrecht stood together at the graveside as the coffin was lowered, shakily, into the grave. The bugler played the last post.

As the long pinewood box touched the bottom of the grave, but before it had completely come to rest, a voice was carried in on the breeze over the heads of the mourners. It was the voice of Baron Munchausen.

"And that was only one of the several occasions on which I met my death. An interesting experience which I don't hesitate strongly to recommend."

Sally's mind was doing somersaults. She closed her eyes tightly and pressed her hands to her face. The voice went on.

"And so, with the help of my inestimable servants, I defeated the Sultan and saved the day."

There was a murmur from the crowd. Sally lowered her

hands and opened her eyes to find herself standing in the theater, on the stage, staring at the profile of the Baron. He was an old man. His dog was beside him. He was addressing the audience in the shell-damaged auditorium.

"And from that time forth, everyone with a talent for it lived happily ever after."

Sally looked around. On the stage with her were the other members of the theater company. Desmond, dressed as Berthold, looking bemused, Jeremy made up to play Gustavus, Bill as Albrecht, Rupert as Adolphus, Rose as Venus. Sally herself, she discovered, was still dressed as one of the Sultan's servants. She blinked hard and shook her head. Had it all really only happened on stage? Someone began to applaud. It was Salt. Sally watched her father as tears rolled down his cheeks. She wanted to run to him. Now the rest of the audience began to clap and cheer. If there'd been a roof on the theater the noise might have lifted it off.

Penetrating through all this came a hard, unpleasant shout, heard at first only by the people at the back of the stalls.

"Stop this nonsense at once!"

Silence spread fast as Horatio Jackson, with Hardy, a group of generals and a company of soldiers moved into the auditorium. Jackson was magenta with rage. He pointed to the Baron.

"You are under arrest for spreading ridiculous tales which have no foundation in truth! Furthermore, you have attempted

to undermine our moral fiber at a time of great danger when the enemy is at the gates! Arrest him!"

Nobody moved. The audience stared at Jackson and the soldiers with evident hostility. Jackson stood up straight and gained a couple of inches.

"I order you to arrest that man!"

One soldier took half a step forward and stopped. Jackson looked as though he might shatter like glass.

"Am I or am I not the Elected Representative?"

Hardy nodded his head madly. Jackson nodded back.

"Arrest him!"

Still nobody moved. Now the Baron climbed down from the stage and, followed by Argus, marched to the exit.

"Open the gates!"

He brandished his stick.

"Open the gates!"

"Open the gates!"

To Sally's amazement, her father, clearly impressed by the Baron, took up the cry and followed him off the stage. Sally, with the rest of the company, joined Salt in pursuit of the Baron.

"Open the gates!"

The audience, too, became enthusiastic for this idea and began to join the general exodus. Jackson could hardly speak for rage.

"Do not open the gates! The Turks are outside and we are not about to surrender!"

By now everyone in the theater had gone, leaving Jackson and his entourage stranded in the middle of the auditorium. He chased after them into the street where many more people were now joining the crowd following the Baron.

"Come back! Stop! I'm warning you! Anybody who opens those gates will be guilty of treason! Arrest that man! Anyone who fails to arrest him is under arrest! And anyone who doesn't arrest them is under arrest!"

Little flecks of spittle were beginning to appear on Jackson's lower lip and chin.

"We will not tolerate a breakdown in law and order at this crucial moment in our history."

Seeing that no one was paying the slightest bit of attention to him, but thinking he could head the Baron off before he reached the main gates, Jackson, his entourage in tow, dived into a side street.


2

Sally half walked and half ran beside the Baron. Behind them most of the townspeople, including some soldiers, had joined the stream of excited people intent on opening the gates.

Word of the power of The Adventures of the Baron Munchausen had spread. Rumor had it that the Baron's tales were so outrageous, and that they required a suspension of disbelief on the part of the audience of such magnitude, that after being exposed to them, nobody and nothing was ever quite the same again. It was said that the Baron's imaginative exertions were so daring in their extravagance that, far from remaining within the realm of the anecdote or the walls of the theater or the covers of a book, they emanated out to affect and change the world at large, and that in this case they had driven away the Sultan.

It should be pointed out that not everybody thought this. Some people believed that the Baron was merely a purveyor of whopping great lies and that he was a pernicious influence who should be kept away from the young.

Sally felt fairly sure she knew what they would discover when they opened the gates.

When the barricaded archway came into view, Jackson, Hardy, five comparatively fit generals and three dozen soldiers raced from a side street and stood, panting for breath, in front of the Baron, effectively blocking his way. Jackson clutched his heaving chest.

"The gates will remain closed!"

The soldiers took up positions across the width of the street. Sally glanced at the Baron. He waved his stick.

"Open the gates!"

His voice was hoarse. Almost inaudible. He coughed violently. Sally's heart sank. The truth was, he was a frail old man. She saw Jackson have the same thought and smile. If the Baron faltered now it would be the end. Behind them, the crowd, sensing hesitation at the front and seeing Jackson's armed soldiers, began to fall back and drift into the side streets. The Baron coughed again. It looked to Sally as though it were all going to dissolve into nothing.

Suddenly, Salt stepped forward.

"Open the gates!"

His powerful voice, honed to a fine pitch on all the crowned heads of Europe, boomed along the street. The retreating crowd stopped and turned back. Sally was thrilled. Jackson went rigid.

"Shoot anyone who disobeys my orders."

The soldiers leveled their muskets at the front of the crowd. Salt strode up to within feet of them.

"Open the gates, dear friends, and seize the day!"

The Baron now drew his sword, saluted Salt and marched on, unhindered, through the line of soldiers. Everyone else began to follow. Jackson was apoplectic.

"Shoot them!"

The soldiers let them pass.

"Stop! Have I not made myself clear? I'll give you one more chance! Shoot these people at once!"

The soldiers turned and joined the crowd, who had begun to clear the barricade from the gates. Jackson stamped his foot.

"This is irrational! You're under arrest! All of you!"

Hardy nodded his head vigorously whereupon Jackson,

frustrated beyond reason, knocked him to the ground. Now a group of children gathered around and began to tease and taunt Jackson, calling him names, laughing at him and hitting him when his back was to them. He tried to catch them, but they dodged away.

"You're under arrest! All of you! I want to see you all outside my office at four o'clock when the bell tolls."

The children ran to watch the gates being opened, leaving Jackson to rant and rave at the wretched Hardy.

## 3

Sally was standing next to the Baron under the great stone archway as Desmond, Bill, Jeremy and Rupert removed the last bolt in the massive iron-studded gates and with the help of others at the front, pulled them slowly back on their hinges.

When the gates had come to rest and their hinges stopped groaning, everyone stood looking out in silence. What they saw was what they had already seen in the Baron's adventure. The Turkish camp was in ruins, the plain was littered with abandoned tents and equipment and the Sultan and his army had gone.

Sally thought again of her father's line in Hamlet. " . . . more things in heaven and earth . . . " It was indeed a rum business.

Everyone cheered and spilled out onto the plain laughing and dancing. Sally was surprised to find herself feeling rather sad and tearful. She wondered what could possibly come next or how anything in the future could fail to be a disappointment. A shrill whistle disturbed her thoughts. She looked around at the Baron to find him with his fingers between his teeth. He gave another piercing blast. Everyone followed the Baron's gaze to beyond the deserted Turkish camp where a small cloud of dust rose from the sand. It grew quickly, getting closer, until a fine white stallion was discernible.

Bucephalus was cheered and applauded as he cantered up to the Baron. The Baron rubbed Bucephalus's nose and neck, put his foot in a stirrup and pulled himself into the saddle. Sally watched. Was he really going to ride away without saying anything to her? The Baron met her gaze. He smiled. Then, putting his hand in his jacket pocket he took out a faded red crumpled paper rose. It was the one intended for Venus. He leaned down and gave it to Sally. She squinted up at him, shading her eyes with her hand.

"It wasn't just a story, was it?"

Sally hadn't really expected an answer and she didn't get one. The Baron smiled, doffed his hat, shook hands with Desmond, Bill, Jeremy and Rupert and rode away with Argus trotting at his side. Once, from the other side of the Turkish camp, he stopped, turned and waved before disappearing over a ridge of sand.

Sally sniffed at the paper rose. It smelled of nothing, or perhaps anything she wanted it to smell of. Salt put his arm around her shoulder.

"So, Henry Salt and Daughter, then?"

Sally hugged him.

"When do we begin?"